AS IT HAPPENS

by

Rukshana Master

To Kirsten,

with best wishes.

Happy reading!

Rukshana

New Generation Publishing

Dedicated with love
to my wonderful family

Jehan,
Jamsheed, Daraius and Becky,

Tatjana, Harrison and Xanthia

and
my sister Feroza

CHAPTERS

Chapter 1: In the Footsteps of Alexander 1

Chapter 2:   Ancestors and Automobiles 17

Chapter 3: Through the Eyes of a Child.....................32

Chapter 4: Reading, 'Riting and 'Rithmetic 40

Chapter 5: Out for a Fling and Ring-a-ding ding 49

Chapter 6: Spreading my Wings 60

Chapter 7: Jehan's Voyage of Discovery 75

Chapter 8: Springing Off with Offspring 91

Chapter 9: Joining Scouting Unprepared!............. 103

Chapter 10: Finding Joumeyrac............................ 114

Chapter 11: French Frolics.................................... 125

Chapter 12: Making new Friends and Meeting a
Count... 135

Chapter 13: The Little Dog Laughed to see Such Fun
.... 150

Chapter 14: Boutique Rukshana 161

Chapter 15: Carcassone, Cathars and the Helicopter
.... 169

Chapter 16: The Wonderful Gorges du Tarn 184

Chapter 17: Soirée Saucisson 192

Chapter 18: Visitors from Leafy Surrey................. 206

Chapter 19: Construction and Deconstruction 221

Chapter 20: French Weddings................................ 237

Chapter 21: Monsieur & Madame B's English
Holiday 253

Chapter 22: Market Day in Millau.............................262

Chapter 23: Rita's Cabin and Barcelona 269

Chapter 24: Le Viaduc et Le Pont du Gard 276

Chapter 25: Tatjana's First Visit to Joumeyrac 290

Chapter 26: Replacing the Roof DIY.........................297

Chapter 27: Finding Pont de la Vinzelle 308

Chapter 28: One House Less in the Aveyron.........320

Preface

Stop for a moment and reflect; how come you are where you are now? Are you able to say "If I die right now, I will die happy"? Well, that's got you thinking. Because, life is like that - brilliant one day and gone the next. So, to quote the famous Scout motto, Be Prepared!

Admittedly, life has been very happy for yours truly, with a colourful, multi-cultural and sunny childhood in India, followed by an eye-opening sojourn in the United States to study fashion design, thanks to Rotary International. True love appeared and after a joyful wedding, more adventures lay in wait on arriving to live in England.

Children came along in due course, and ever intrepid, the buying of a ramshackle *maison de vigne* in France, with no electricity or running water. A holiday project, which became a major part of our lives, it brought lots of hilarious pleasure. Joining the 1st Claygate Scout Group, with wet and cold camps and riotous Group shows and then changing character to run a hugely successful fashion business has been challenging. Organising many Fashion shows for charities over the years and several Music Festivals, always together as a family, life has been an exhilarating rollercoaster. It was all about turning the dips into risers and making a bad situation happy.

Our ancestors and their genes must contribute to how we look at life – there are some good stories of humour, adventure and recklessness there, too. These traits are now appearing in the grandchildren.... whose fault was that, I wonder?

Read on and you might discover what *you* could have been responsible for!

Chapter 1: In the Footsteps of Alexander

As it happens, the saying, 'There's nowt so queer as folk' is absolutely true. We all look at life differently, we all handle situations in a different way and, in spite of all our differences, we expect other people to think and behave in the same way we do. This is not possible, as each of us is the product of our genes and our own particular upbringing and education. This makes for a very interesting world and it also means that each one of us has a distinctly unique story to tell. This is mine.

The day I was born my parents took delivery of their very first motor car - a turquoise blue Hillman with red leather seats. It was the 4th of May 1949 and I will never know which caused more excitement at 7 Mangaldas Road in Poona, India. A few days before I was due to be born, my mother went to the cinema to see an Indian blockbuster movie called 'Sikandar', which was all about Alexander the Great and his conquests. Sikandar was the name the Indians gave him – perhaps it sounded like Alexander to them. She was so enamoured with the handsome actor who played the title role, that she decided I would be called 'Sikandar', assuming I would be a boy. She came home from the movies and, apparently, ran around the house in her nightshirt, heavily pregnant, waving her arms about in victory, shouting 'Sikandar! Sikandar!' as his army had done. Well, I duly arrived, but without the necessary tackle for a Sikandar. So, Sikand-best, (sorry) she named me Rukshana, after the Persian princess Alexander married and carried off. Thank goodness I wasn't a boy.

As I was born into a Parsi family, it might help to explain briefly at this point just who the Parsis are. The Parsis arrived in India over 1000 years ago, and there is a lovely little story attached to this. To escape persecution from the wave of Islamic fervour that threatened to destroy their way of life in Persia, three shiploads of Zoroastrians fled to India. They were followers of the Prophet Zoroaster, practicing a wonderfully natural science of respecting the Sun and all the elements of nature. When they arrived on the shores of Gujerat, on the west coast of India, requesting shelter, the King of that state refused them permission to stay, sending as his reply a glass of milk, full to the brim. This was to say 'My country is full, we have no room for you.' The leader of the people from Pars (Persia) sprinkled a tiny pinch of sugar on the milk. The sugar dissolved instantly. This was his way of saying 'There are so few of us to so many of you. We can only sweeten your lives by being here.' The King was so impressed that he allowed them to stay and gave them land to build their homes. He also made them promise to respect Indian customs and never to try to convert his people. The Parsis were more concerned about losing their own identity in this hugely populated country, so they happily settled in India. From those humble beginnings, the Parsis became leading industrialists, philanthropists and a highly respected part of Indian society.

My parents had come to live in this enormous mansion, the year before I came along, at the request of its owner, a very wealthy doctor from Bombay whose country home it was. With the house came eleven acres of land planted with fruit orchards, a lovely rose garden and every tropical plant you can think of. Being a very busy man he hardly ever had time to enjoy all this and the house was empty most of the time.

Around that time, soon after India had gained its independence from British rule, there was much talk of large, unoccupied properties being commandeered by the Army to house their personnel, so this wily gentleman decided to set about finding a trustworthy, reliable and deserving young couple to occupy the first floor. My father's reputation, as a hardworking and bright young man with a young family (my sister Feroza), had come to his attention, and one fine morning in 1948 a grand horse-drawn carriage drew up outside their humble abode in Main Street. A distinguished Parsi gentleman in a black frock coat and top hat stepped out and made them an offer they couldn't refuse.

Dad insisted on paying rent, so a minimal amount was agreed (probably all they could afford), and they moved into their very large and wonderful new home with two chairs, three plates and a large saucepan. Or so the story went.

The approach to the house was via a long driveway through very large green gates from the main road. There was also another driveway through a second set of gates in the side road. A sweeping wooden staircase led to the first floor, which opened on to a wide verandah with a black and white marble floor. This led into an enormous hall, with a ceiling so high that the huge crystal chandelier, which was eight feet long, seemed quite modest. The bedrooms were on either side of the hall with doorways at least nine feet high. At the other end, the hall opened up onto another verandah and a large balcony above the porch. The flooring throughout the main rooms was honeycomb terracotta tile, with the bathrooms in white marble. A grand place, to be sure and, no doubt, took my gentle parents a bit of getting used to.

However, their luck continued to improve and by the time I arrived, with a silver spoon in my mouth, all was wonderful. My mother's family was reasonably well to do - she was one of several children. My maternal grandmother (née Tehmina Mugaseth) was born in Rawalpindi, which is now in Pakistan. She was only 14 years old when she married and had her first child. I believe she lost two children but two boys and five girls survived into old age - one of whom was my mother, Mani Cama. My maternal grandfather Jamshedji was born in London, as his father was a merchant with the East India Company and lived in Kensington. The Cama ancestors were very well known Parsi philanthropists and industrialists.

Thanks to the legacy of the British Empire, my sister and I went to the best schools possible. We really did have the finest teachers who had been sent out to India to educate the English children living there and had then stayed on after British rule ended. The first school I attended was St. Mary's Convent in Poona. I remember my nursery school teacher, Mrs. Aitken and her son Eric, with a mop of golden curls – he was probably my first heartthrob. I also recall weeing in my pants and having my bloomers washed and put out to dry in a corner of the playground. It is quite possible to be embarrassed at the age of four, especially if you're in love. St. Mary's was run entirely by nuns, who wore long black habits down to the floor, and as their heads were completely covered with veil and wimpole, I had no way of telling whether they were male or female – especially as some of them had a liberal sprinkling of whiskers and wore sturdy black boots.

We learned more about English and European history than Indian and I developed a great love of the English language, Shakespeare, Wordsworth and all the rest. Hindi and Marathi (the local language) were compulsory and French was also included. Mathematics became terribly complicated because we had to learn all about Pounds, Shillings and Pence and then convert the sums into Indian currency, that being Rupees and Annas – both systems being Imperial and totally illogical. It might help to explain things if I told you that there were 12 pence to one shilling, 20 shillings to one pound in the British system and 16 annas to 1 rupee in the Indian system. Then again, maybe that wouldn't help at all. India then went metric. However, we still had to do the sums! Why, I will never know, because India did not use pounds, shillings and pence.....this has scarred my ability to understand maths for life. The only high spot of the maths lesson was Sister Cora, our teacher, who was highly entertaining to watch as she had the most enormous yellow protruding teeth which moved alarmingly each time she spoke.

The school bus came to fetch me everyday. I had to be at the gates at the end of the long drive early in the morning – my ayah sat with me till the bus arrived. We watched the bullock-carts trundling past on their way to town, laden with farm produce for the market. Mornings were often cold and misty and with the house being surrounded by wilderness and greenery, we often heard jackals howling in the woods. The ancient green school bus would clatter into sight, having picked up several children from their homes, and in I would climb – girls down one side, boys down the other. St. Mary's was a girls' school but right next door was Bishop's, which was only for boys. Separating the two was a low brick wall. This made for an interesting life. There was hardly any traffic on the roads then and I'm not even sure if our bus driver had a driving licence. Still, we got to school relatively unharmed except for the paper pellets shot from rubber bands at the girls by the boys.

The high spot of the primary school day was Lunchtime. Tables would be set out in the shade of the enormous Banyan trees in the playground. Some children brought packed lunches, but many of us had a hot lunch delivered to us everyday. This would arrive in a tiffin-carrier (a stack of three tins held together by a clamp). One tin would contain rice, another curry and the third, some vegetables. A dessert would also be secreted somewhere. Miraculously, all would arrive hot and in perfect time for lunch with, wait for it, a plate, knives, forks, spoons and a white damask table-napkin. Some girls even had a tablecloth. How did it all get there - you ask. On a bicycle, of course – slung on the handlebars and expertly balanced all the way from home (three miles away) by one of the young men in our employ. He then cleared everything away and took it home.

This practice still continues in modern-day Mumbai, where the office workers in the city have their lunches delivered by the Dabbawallas (lunch-box men) every single day. They collect from various homes and deliver to the correct offices without so much as a sat-nav. Absolutely amazing – on bicycles, no less. All arrives hot and fresh in spite of chaotic traffic, cows in the middle of the road and drivers with no regard for traffic lights (when they worked). What is more, these chaps balance up to fifty tiffin carriers on one bicycle and ride it, of course. I kid you not. This is an extraordinary talent, which puts riding a bike onto a whole new level. Perhaps they should make an Olympic sport of it.

My sister, Feroza, was six years older than me (still is, amazingly) and was already in secondary school when I was six, so we had a different set of friends and interests. I was probably a real thorn in her side as I was also a bit of a spoilt brat. Actually, she was the lively one most likely to .get into trouble and I was the canny one who watched her being chastised and realised what not to do. There is much to be learnt by simple observation and the second child has an advantage, as parents are much more relaxed the second time round. I adored my older sister and followed her around like a lap dog. Whatever she suggested, I did, including asking for her favourite choice of gift for my birthday! She was hugely musical (still is), and I owe most of my musical knowledge to her interest in all the latest releases. We would listen to the 'Binaca Hit Parade', which was relayed by a radio station sponsored by a brand of green toothpaste, and rock to Elvis and Bill Haley. There was a music shop called 'Apollo' in Main Street that stocked hundreds of LPs and singles. We spent hours in there, listening to everything and buying nothing, until it was my birthday.

Before we had a modern hi-fi system, my parents had a wind-up gramophone and lots of classical records. Controlling the volume on the wind-up was by shoving a duster down the sound hole. Feroza also taught me how to ride a bicycle. What she didn't teach me was how to use the brakes. On the old bikes, you squeezed the brakes on the left handlebar first, which slowed the rear wheel and then the ones on the right handlebar, which slowed the front. If you squeezed hard only on the right, while rolling downhill, you went head over heels over the handlebars. Fact.

Feroza   Mum   Me

Each of us had an Ayah to ourselves. Ayahs always wore white saris and were there all the time, looking after our every need. They were kind and gentle, smelled of washing soap and cloves and put up with a lot of nonsense from us. Our clothes were neatly ironed and laid out for us every morning, our beds were made and our shoes polished.

My mother never went to work in her life. The most arduous task of the day would be to decide what to order Cook to prepare for lunch and dinner. This ceremony would take place each morning at the dining table, after breakfast. Cook would arrive with his little book to take notes. Mother would suggest some exotic dish involving unusual ingredients, and he would say 'But Madam, it is out of season!' and she would say 'That's nonsense, just find some' and he'd say 'Well, it will cost a lot more than what you give me to spend' and she'd say 'Nonsense, you know you can manage' and the poor man would somehow produce the most fantastic meals on what one would consider a shoestring. It was no wonder that he drank heavily. One evening he turned to our dog (called Tensing as he was a Tibetan terrier) and said 'Here Johnny-Johnny, here, Johnny, Johnny!' and Mum said 'His name's not Johnny – you're drunk!' So quick as a flash he replied ' I *know* his name's not Johnny but *today* I am calling him Johnny'.

When I think about it, there were no academies for cooks or Masterchef classes in those days. This man was from an ordinary family from Goa and lived, with his wife Mary and two small children, in one of the little cottages at the bottom of the garden, which we called the servants quarters. Yet, his culinary talents were extraordinary. He could make baskets out of fine threads of caramel, fill them with fruit salad and cream and then put a caramel handle over the top. He made the most delicate soufflés and cakes and was brilliant with Indian, Parsi and European dishes. All this was accomplished on an earthenware cooker, which was fired by coal, including the oven. Truly amazing. This was the reason my parents tolerated the drinking. It clearly helped him concentrate.

Milk was delivered to the house every morning in the form of a water buffalo. She would be milked under my mother's watchful eye (to ensure that no water had been added to the milk). The large pail of milk would then be boiled thoroughly and left to cool. After a night in the refrigerator, the cream would be skimmed off – it was two inches thick – and we would eat it with bananas and extra sugar as a treat after school. Or, indeed, just on its own. Buffalo milk was much richer than cow's milk, but more readily available.

There were two gardeners (Big Mali and Small Mali) who brought fresh flowers up for us everyday and watered a hundred terracotta pots of roses. Roses would not grow in the ground there, so they had to be lovingly potted up and nurtured. I loved spending time with the gardeners and learning about all the different plants including orchids, which they would plant in moss on the tree trunks. There were papaya trees and a very large mango tree in the orchard and bougainvillea everywhere in the brightest colours. The wife of one of the gardeners came to clean the house everyday. There were no vacuum cleaners, so she had to sweep miles of tiled floor and wash one room each day with a mild disinfectant. The beds were high off the ground so they had to be cleaned underneath daily to keep mosquitoes and other mites at bay.

Then, there was the man whose sole job it was to clean the toilets. This job was considered beneath anyone else. The Hindus in India had a strict caste system, something I have never been able to understand. So he went to everybody's house in turn to do only this. He was called the Mether. Nobody appreciated his talent very much but the day he did not turn up was a major catastrophe! Three cheers for the Mether, albeit a bit late.

Washing machines did not exist in India at that time so we had a Dhobi who would come once a week to take the dirty laundry and replace it with clean and beautifully ironed sheets and towels – all washed in the river and ironed with coal heated irons. Considering they took the laundry from several homes – neatly tied up in separate bags – nothing ever went missing or got mixed up. The form of transport was a bicycle. Can you picture a man riding a bicycle while balancing ten large bags of washing – some clean, some dirty? (Another idea for the Olympics). These are the true heroes of this world and they go completely unnoticed. There was such a retinue of staff that I suppose my mother had her hands full just organising them. It was not a bad life and there were lots of parties, as my parents had a huge circle of friends.

Mum was a very good tennis player, with a cabinet full of trophies for various tournaments she had won. She would take me with her to the Poona Club and while she was on the tennis courts, I would spend time in the library, devouring every book I could lay my hands on. From Enid Blyton to PG Wodehouse, I read anything. The aroma and feel of old books is still exciting.

All our clothing was made by a tailor (Darjee). Ready - made clothing did not exist, so you went along to *'The Imperial Hosiery'* and chose some dress material, (the smell of cotton fabric still brings on the anticipation of pretty new frocks) and took it to the tailor, who was called Laxman. He used to sit cross-legged on the floor and operate his sewing machine with a hand wheel. He did eventually progress to a treadle machine and finally electricity, but the confections he created, simply from looking at pictures out of American or English fashion magazines, were incredible. Ready-to-use dress patterns had not been invented so how did this man make clothes that fitted perfectly with immaculate detail? Who taught him to produce such haute couture without any Fashion Design colleges or courses available? Fittings were complicated as, being a man, he had to make the garment up to a level at which it was respectable to try on before he could make any adjustments. Zip fasteners and buttons had to be in place for a fitting. Which meant that he had double the amount of work unpicking everything. As a fully-fledged dressmaker, I appreciate his art a thousand-fold. He did not have the luxury of ready-made dress patterns and the fit was always perfect.

India was, and still is, full of people like that – craftsmen and women who have had their art handed down through generations and adept at creating and copying anything. From delicate watch mechanisms to engine components, if they couldn't get it, they made it. Hence the thriving industry of imitation designer goods!

Grandpa Jamshedji & Grandma Tehmina 1904

Mum & Dad (Mani & Nozer Homji) 1940

Chapter 2: Ancestors and Automobiles

One member of staff my parents did not indulge in was a chauffeur, or 'Driver' as he was properly called. This was because both my parents loved driving, especially my mother. There must have been something genetic about this as her mother was the first Indian woman to enter a motor race from Poona to Satara in 1906. She came first, of course, and I still have the silver Aga Khan Challenge Cup she won. The car she drove had a crank handle to start it up. She drove all the way to Satara, a distance of some sixty-two miles, turned around and came back, mercifully without stalling or turning the engine off, as the crank handle had been left on the ground at the starting post. Unmade roads, stones and dust flying, a woman in a man's world wearing a sari, all her best jewellery, soft shoes and silk stockings.....wow!

Grandmother Tehmina Cama after winning the Aga Khan Challenge Cup 1906

In England, around the same time – 1908 to be precise – my great-great grandmother was driving herself to Windsor Castle, in her newly acquired automobile, to be presented to King Edward VII and Queen Alexandra. Her name was Dosebai Jessawalla and she was, possibly, the first Indian (and Parsi) woman to drive a car in England. She writes about the event in her fascinating book 'The Story of my Life'. She was from a very forward thinking family, and became one of the first Indian (Parsi) women to attend an English school. Being from a rather affluent family herself and then having married a very wealthy widower three times her age, she got to travel the world and had friends in high places, including the British nobility. She made a voyage round the world, including Japan, Hawaii and on to the United States. She saw traces of the great San Francisco earthquake of 1906, visited Washington DC and the White House, Pennsylvania, the Niagara Falls and of course, New York.

It makes me weak at the knees whenever I read her book. She has been my inspiration to write. At the end of her world trip, she left New York on the steamship 'St Paul' and arrived in Southampton after an eight-day crossing. Once back in London, she set about achieving her life's ambition.

That was why, at the tender age of 76, she bought herself a motorcar and drove it for the first time from London to Windsor, accompanied by her stepson. They broke down on the way there and were helped by some 'gentle folk'.

The indomitable Dosebai Cawasjee Jessawalla in her younger days.

She got there in good time and presented the Queen with a heavily embroidered dress decoration encrusted with rubies and emeralds and pure gold embroidery. To the King, she presented a carved wooden casket set with miniature paintings of her own family and also that of their Majesties, along with a richly embellished cap set with miniatures of the King and Queen and several precious stones. We have photographs of the gifts to the Royal couple, and I have contacted the Royal Archives Collection at Windsor to see if they can be located. The Archivists have sent me a copy of the *Court Circular* of the 20th June 1908 describing the event exactly as she had in her book. In due course, I hope the gifts will be tracked down and what joy it will be to see them. They were all her very own handiwork.

We had a string of interesting cars, thanks to my mother's fascination for them. In the days before I was born she rode Dad's motorbike. One of the cars I clearly remember was a large black Citroen (Traction Avant), which regularly caught fire when you started it up because it backfired. This was quite alarming, but not for my mother. She would calmly open up the long bonnet and beat the flames out with a hessian sack carried in the car just for that purpose. Then we'd be on our way – second time lucky. Then there was something called a Ford Zephyr, which was huge, black and belched fumes in all directions. She even borrowed a metallic blue, left hand drive Cadillac convertible from some wealthy friends for a while. It takes great skill to drive anywhere in India. Theoretically, one drives on the left, but in practice, one drives wherever there is a space. Horns are absolutely essential, if only to have something to grab on to for security. Cows take priority over cars, of course, and seeing one sitting in the middle of the road is considered a privilege. Most taxis also have sound-assisted reversing, which means they play 'Happy Birthday' or 'Colonel Bogie' very loudly while reversing. Terribly sensible, or just plain terrible.

In 1933, when my mother was seventeen and had just passed her driving test, her father retired from service in the Customs and Excise Department. Her mother, Tehmina, promptly suggested that they all drive up to Srinagar in the mountain state of Kashmir, high up in the Himalayas. She thought it would be a fantastic family adventure to live on a houseboat for a couple of months, on the stunningly beautiful Lake Dal, surrounded by the fabulous gardens laid out by the Mughal Emperors over 300 years earlier. Although Kashmir is about 2,500 miles away from Poona, the distance did not worry my grandmother. There were several drivers in the family and they could all take turns. There would be seven of them travelling – my grandmother (Mama), my grandfather (Papa), Uncle Pilloos (who was a bit of a mystery character who lived with the family, was very rich and had a stammer), my mother, her brother Naval who was an expert mechanic and their two younger sisters who, I imagine, had been excused from school.

This being such a grand and courageous (if not foolhardy), undertaking, meticulous details had to be worked out. Roads were unmade and almost non-existent, there were no petrol stations or service stops on the way and certainly no pubs to take a break in. The plan was to camp overnight, but not camping the way we know it. To start with, they bought a brand new 7-seater Hudson car from Ms.Kandawalla & Co., the biggest car dealers in those days. It was fitted out with special boxes, roof racks, plenty of spare tyres, tubes and all the mechanical equipment they might need. Also, rifles and shotguns, which were *de rigeur* as hunting game was quite acceptable, not to mention the bandits they might meet along the way.

For the camping equipment another large vehicle was specially constructed for them – a customized van on an old Dodge chassis. This was fitted out with sleeping berths, water tanks and conveniences for overnight stays in the forests. Extra fuel would also have been carried somehow. Cooking utensils, huge quantities of tinned food, camping stoves, lanterns – just thinking about this makes me dizzy. It was a journey into the unknown. The driving was shared among Mama, Uncle Pilloos, my mother and Naval, as Papa did not drive. They had also chosen a delightful and strong Sikh driver to take charge of the van. His name was Avtar Singh. One sunny morning in March they set off.

In 1933 India was still under the British Raj and Pakistan did not exist. India was not one united country as it is today, but a collection of assorted states, some ruled directly by Indian rulers and some under British rule. There were even tiny city states, with very few inhabitants. The laws and customs of each state were different according to the religions and beliefs of the rulers. There were Hindu Rajas, Muslim Nawabs, Sikh Sardars and the like. Travellers passing through had to observe and respect the laws of wherever they were.

In Hindu states, beef was prohibited as the cow is considered sacred, whilst in Muslim states, pork was strictly taboo. At each border crossing, the Customs guards checked the labels on each can of food (mostly imported from England) and simply destroyed whatever was not allowed. One could lose one's entire supply this way, so, having wised up to this fact earlier, they removed all the labels from all the tins. This made for some interesting meals but at least they still had something left to eat!

One morning, they saw a beautiful peacock in a deserted clearing in the forest, just outside a village. Naval decided he would shoot it and they could have it for dinner. So he took a pot shot, missed, and the next thing they saw was a large crowd of angry villagers charging at them waving sticks and baying for their blood. The peacock is also a sacred bird (and even if it wasn't, how daft can you be)? so the family found themselves in big trouble. Luckily for them, their gallant Sikh driver came to the rescue and calmed the villagers down. They never found out what he said to them but it worked and they managed to drive away unharmed. This was a close call.

They continued on their amazing journey north, driving through various cities, villages and thick forest. There were several punctures to contend with thanks to the numerous metal 'shoes' from the bullock carts that used the same tracks, and the odd mechanical breakdown. Now and again they would stop at a 'Dak' bungalow. These were Government rest houses meant for touring officers and also for the use of the postal messengers, running or riding out with the Post (Dak) night and day. This postal system was replaced after the railways were built, around 1860 onwards.

The 'Dak' bungalows were always in the middle of nowhere, surrounded by forests and wild animals. Light was provided by kerosene lamps and bath water heated on log fires. I have nostalgic memories of staying in them when the family accompanied my father on one of his field trips. The smell of wood smoke and the kerosene lamps brings back warm, happy days.

I do not have a detailed diary of this historic journey but can only guess at their route north. They would have travelled via Ahmadabad to Jodhpur in Rajasthan and continued through wild country alternating between forests rich with game and dry stony desert with very little civilization and a few goats for company. Bikaner would have been on their route and almost certainly Rawalpindi, as that is where Grandmother was born. Here the true account continues – they headed for the North-West Frontier and the infamous Khyber Pass.

This Pass in the Himalayas has been the gateway into India for umpteen raiders, marauders, conquerors and settlers from various regions of Central Asia and Europe over thousands of years – Alexander the Great and the many Mughal Emperors to name a few. It is now a corridor between Afghanistan and Pakistan, and just as dangerous and unpredictable as it has always been. As Pakistan did not exist in 1933, the border was guarded by Indian troops.

On reaching the North West Frontier, they were surrounded by wild looking Afridy tribesmen, brandishing rifles and bristling with loaded cartridge belts, not to mention the curved daggers on their hips. However, they were not as threatening as they looked and, under the watchful eyes of the Indian soldiers (Jawans), they crowded round the Hudson car patting its polished surface and poking its fat tyres. Silent and suspicious, their manners changed instantly when Grandfather asked if they were in 'Pakhtoonistan,' which was the name they dearly desired to call this area if ever granted independence. The magic word brought smiles and gestures of friendship but one did not wish to push one's luck. The family posed for photographs with the Jawans, and uncle Pilloos tried to impress the tribesmen that he was a VIP while twirling his impressive moustache. With a prudent hint from the Army Corporal not to linger amongst these unpredictable firebrands, they turned back and headed for Murree on the way to Srinagar.

The Murree Pass leads directly to Srinagar and forms part of the line dividing present day India and Pakistan.

Thus they entered Srinagar. The sight that greeted them was spectacular. There were vast gardens and canals laid out for miles and miles. Designed by Persian architects commissioned by the great Mughal Emperors of

India in the 16th and 17th Centuries, they were primarily laid out as pleasure playgrounds and summer retreats for the Royals to escape the extreme heat of Delhi and the plains. However, there was a practical use for this, too. When the ice of the Himalayan mountain range melted in summer, it opened the roads for raiders, freebooters, Afridy tribesmen and even organised armies from the north to pour into Kashmir and grab this lovely land. So the Mughal Kings discreetly moved their armies to these summer frontiers, while ostentatiously holidaying in this paradise.

Paradise, no doubt, it is, as any visitor even today would testify. It was 400 years ago that a court poet composed the immortal lines 'Agar behesht ber rue zamin hast, hamin hast, hamin hast, hamin hast' – 'If Paradise be on the face of this Earth, this is it, this is it, this is it'. These words are carved into a marble tablet in the Royal Court at Agra, but refer to Srinagar.

The most pleasurable thing about Srinagar was living in a houseboat on the great Dal Lake and moving from place to place as you pleased. It was exciting to be in a floating home, complete with bedrooms, kitchen and bath, lazing on rich Persian carpets on the verandahs while gliding majestically on the lake or down one of the quiet canals that formed a labyrinth around the lake. Or you could stay put in some shady bower of your choice for days on end as the icy cold waters of the Himalayas flowed past.

The houseboat lifestyle was introduced by the British, who had come to rule India about two hundred years earlier. Following the end of the Mughal period, Kashmir was ruled by a Hindu Maharaja, who would not permit any outsiders to own land or build houses in Kashmir. The British visitors respected this ruling but cleverly circumvented the law by building floating houses on the water.

The houseboat they rented was called 'The Lion's Lair' and it was their home for two months. It was owned by an enterprising man called Rahim Khan who was friend, philosopher, cook and butler with enough experience to handle the eccentricities of visitors from all parts of the world. He produced magnificent meals cooked on board with the freshest ingredients. Imagine the ecstasy of lying on cushions on a moonlit night on the lake, surrounded by water lilies and listening to the water lapping the side of the boat.

Native Kashmiris had an amazing capacity to withstand the cold. They had to live here long after the tourists had gone back to warmer climes and the lake was freezing over. No central heating and not much shelter in a wooden hut. But their ingenuity knew no bounds and they tied earthen pots filled with hot coals round their stomachs, which kept their entire systems warm. During summer, however, hordes of them would jump into the icy cold water early every morning for their daily baths. My grandmother, ever adventurous and thinking 'how bad could that be' got it into her head to try the same. One morning the family awoke to find her in her swimming costume ready for a dip. They watched in disbelief as she jumped in nonchalantly as the rest of them shivered in horror. Needless to say, she waded out as fast as she had entered with 'never again' written all over her face. But she did it!

The time came to leave Paradise and go home. I am grateful that someone took the trouble to write an account of what must have been an epic adventure so that I could share it with you.

Grandma Tehmina and Grandpa Jamshedji in 1904.

Mum & Dad with their Royal Enfield in 1947

Chapter 3: Through the Eyes of a Child

My Dad had humble beginnings. His father was a Tax Collector and spent many months away from home touring remote areas of Northern India on horseback, as tax collecting was exactly what it said, going from village to village being thoroughly unpopular and perpetually in danger of being mugged. Being a British Civil Servant, he was reasonably well paid but his children hardly ever saw him. Add to that, my father's mother, Amy, died when he was just 6 years old, leaving him and his two siblings to be brought up by her sister's family. On the bright side, my father was extraordinarily intelligent and had the personality to charm a lion away from its kill. This gained him a scholarship to Engineering College while studying for a Law degree at the same time.

He started school at Dastur's, which was then only for Parsi students and lessons were held in Gujerati with English as a second language. In spite of this, he was soon adept at tackling the Times crossword puzzle. He spoke Persian, Hindi and Marathi and was a brilliant mathematician. He also played the drums in the Territorial Army Band – oh, and the flute, sometimes. Dad was a self-made man in more ways than one – he changed his name from Nozer Hormasji Hathidaru to Nozer Homji as soon as he came of age – simpler and much less of a mouthful. His siblings retained the original surname but never had any offspring, and as he had two daughters, his name remained unique. After graduation, with a degree in Engineering and also a Law degree after his name, his life took quite a different turn. He was introduced, by a friend, to the latest arrival in the business world – 'Life Insurance.' With the gift of the gab and the most engaging personality ever, he became an agent for the Sun Life Corporation of India, selling life insurance premiums to wealthy businessmen, who would have otherwise had to pay huge taxes on their profits. This was a much wiser investment, by far! Over the years he climbed to the top of his tree, becoming one of India's leading experts on finance.

He met my mother while she was very young and they had a fairly clandestine relationship to start with – though with her family of four sisters and two brothers nothing was secret for very long. Her mother was extremely strict (she had to be, to keep that lot under control). My mother's eldest sister had already been disowned as she ran away with one of the most notorious playboys in town. Not a big deal now, but at that time it was a major disgrace to the family. Her father forgave her but her mother never spoke to her again. This made my mother very sad, as she adored her eldest sister. Thank goodness times have changed. My parents married in 1940 and my sister was born in 1943.

The weather in Poona was totally predictable. For nine months of the year there was sunshine – hot and dry, and then three months of Monsoon rain – torrential downpours with spectacular thunderstorms and flooding. The start of the Monsoon was always an exciting time with rumbles of thunder which went on for days before it finally broke, and we all rushed out to stand in the rain to cool off. After the initial euphoria the novelty wore off as the roof began to leak, the garden flooded and there was misery as landslides washed away huts in the villages and roads became impassable. However, the rain was most welcome for the farmers and, of course, the cricket greens and the racecourse. The racing season would start at the end of the Monsoon and Poona had its own renowned Royal Western India Turf Club with a grand racecourse. Horses and jockeys from all over the world would come to race there and it was big business. It is still going strong.

A cloudy day in the hot season would be an unexpected treat and if it happened to arrive at a weekend, it almost certainly meant a picnic. This was no ordinary picnic with a few sandwiches but a full blown affair with lots of friends and several cars, enough food to feed a small country and a long drive out of town into the wilderness. My parents knew how to have a good time. On warm moonlit nights they would go down to the Boat Club with friends and their children and tie three punts together, take all sorts of delicious things to eat and have a moonlight picnic on the river. These were a rare treat and terrific fun.

Dust was everywhere. One just grew up with it. That didn't stop us polishing our shoes like mirrors (did I say us)? I meant some other kind person polishing our shoes for us. My Ayah would iron my uniform and lay everything out every morning to get me ready for school while the Cook prepared a full English breakfast, bar the bacon because that was too much of a luxury for everyday. Needless to say, I was a plump child and grew into a fairly plump teenager and so forth, but very strong, with an immune system to match. This was probably the result of eating anything and everything, even the things we were forbidden to touch, like the bright pink and dubiously flavoured strawberry ices peddled by 'Pop' (because he looked like Popeye the Sailor Man) on his bicycle wagon and sold for one paisa.

Age 6 as (Annie Get Your Gun)

Some evenings we would walk down to the Bund Gardens by the river and snack on all sorts of amazing things sold at the roadside stalls. Some were safe, like the roasted sweetcorn and roasted chickpeas (channa) and some were taboo but delicious. One of these was 'Bhel puri' – perfectly innocuous in itself as it was made with puffed rice, peanuts, chickpeas and bits of boiled potato dressed in a delicious sweet-sour sauce. However, the chap who put it all together looked like he had never washed his hands in his life. He wiped them on a filthy rag between customers and then proceeded to take your order. Then he would fashion a bowl out of a large leaf into which he would scoop a handful of each of the dry ingredients. Finally, the sauce would also be scooped up by hand and the same hand would mix everything together, after which he would top it with a large 'puri' (a sort of biscuit) for you to eat it with. In spite of my mother warning us that he probably hadn't washed his hands after visiting the toilet – we ate the stuff and it was amazing.

Having said all that, I did contract a horrid virus called para-typhoid when I was eight years old and was seriously ill. It must have been pretty awful because most of my hair fell out and I was confined to bed for what seemed like weeks. All I remember of it (apart from the hair) was having a whale of a time playing with my paper dolls, being given loads of American comics and having my mother's undivided attention – come to think of it, she must have been worried sick. As I got better, she used some vile red hair oil of

Ayurvedic origin to restore my hair and it grew back thicker and darker than it had ever been.

I had my Navjote ceremony soon after, when I was nine. My special frock was pale lemon yellow taffeta and tulle net, hand-embroidered by my mother with blue forget-me-nots. The Navjote is an initiation into Zoroastrianism, which is the religion of the Parsis, brought to India from Persia. It is a Dualism which believes in a Power of Good (Ahura Mazda) and a power of Evil (Ahreman). The whole ethos of the religion is the conquest of Good over Evil. Pretty straightforward. Good Thoughts (Humata), Good Words (Hukhta) and Good Deeds (Hvarshta) and Bob's your uncle. It is a very intelligent religion and very difficult to stick to – but how simple to understand. The elements of Air, Fire, Earth and Water are to be revered and respected. This means you do not pollute or abuse these and you look after your planet. The gravitational and magnetic influence of the planets and the Moon, on all plant and human life, was already known to the ancient

Zoroastrians. Most important of all, they knew that the Sun was the centre of our Universe long before Galileo and co. had the idea.

There is also the theory of Thought Vibration – sending out pure thoughts, which will in turn generate good vibrations back to you. We know of the existence of radio and sound waves now, but this was ancient knowledge. The Zoroastrian prayers were written in Avesta, which was not a spoken language but one in which the words carried good vibrations. Hence, they were always said aloud. Over the centuries, with all the transcribing into various phonetics of language they must have lost some of their potency. However, there are plenty of Zoroastrians with firm faith in the power of the 'Ashem Vohu' and the 'Yatha Ahu Vairyo'.

The Navjote ceremony is performed on a stage prettily decorated with flowers. Two priests (Dasturjis) perform the investiture ceremony of the Sadra and Kusti on the child. The Sadra, which is a vest made of fine white muslin, has a tiny pocket sewn into the front (symbolically for your good deeds) and a larger pocket sewn into the back (you guessed it – for your bad deeds)! The Kusti is woven from 72 strands of pure new wool and is very long. It is tied around the waist while saying your prayers and is supposed to be worn by good Zoroastrians day and night to protect you from harm. Of course, the power of your mind and your own good thoughts are more efficient than any physical accouterments, but for too many people the outward show affects the inner self and is an essential part of their being. This is true of most religions.

As with all Zoroastrian/Parsi ceremonies, a huge feast is involved. For the two hundred or so guests, long tables and chairs are set out, under the beautifully lit up trees, and covered with white tablecloths. Huge banana leaves are used as dinner plates and although you can ask for a fork and spoon, the tradition would be to eat with your hands, having of course, washed them first. The first course might be fish, traditionally pomfret, cooked in a delicious sauce of coriander and cream, with chapatis. This would be followed by chicken with apricots, slow-cooked with garlic, ginger, cardamom, cumin and coriander seed topped with crispy potato straws. Then there would certainly be a rice dish with a lamb dahl. All this would be followed by amazing desserts – usually fresh mango icecream or a kulfi (double cream pistachio icecream). Finally, the waiters would arrive with hot water and soap for you to wash your hands.

After the dinner, there was the dancing. We had our own Parsi version of Victor Sylvester's orchestra, in the form of Goody Seervai and his Band. There was a rumour that Strauss' Blue Danube Waltz was the Parsi National Anthem because everyone immediately stood up (to dance) when it was played.

Chapter 4: Reading, 'Riting and 'Rithmetic

Having always been regarded as a race apart, the Parsis were the first to adopt the English language, customs and a more western way of life when India went under British rule. Having said that, some of the leading figures in gaining India's independence in 1947 were also Parsis. I guess they always knew how to be on the winning side at the right time. I could make mention here of another illustrious ancestor, Madame Bhikaiji Rustom Cama. She had been exiled from India as a freedom fighter, and was living in Paris when, she was invited to Stuttgart in Germany, by the famous French Socialist, Jean Jaures, to attend the International Socialist Congress.

To make the best of this opportunity, she designed the first Indian flag, hastily made from three strips of her saris, which she took with her to the Congress in Stuttgart, Germany, on the 22nd of August 1907. India was very much under British rule and as such, not represented as a separate country. She made a fiery speech for the Independence of India and then boldly unfurled her home made flag saying 'This is the flag of free India', much to the admiration of the Germans and the French who were always happy to assist in anything anti-British at the time! The entire event is chronicled in the Stuttgart archives. She returned to India in 1936 but died before India gained independence. Some called her the Indian Joan of Arc and post-independence, she became a national heroine. There are now several roads named after her and also a postage stamp in her honour.

Madame Bhikaiji Cama with the first flag of India

I do not think my great - great grandmother and she ever came into contact as they were at completely opposite poles in their opinions of the British Raj!

The next few years flew by with school and holidays in Bombay with my cousins Rashna, Ketayun and Noshir. My Aunty Zarine had a boutique in her large mansion of a home, where she sold her own designs in children's clothes and babywear. It was a hugely successful business and as there was a busy workshop full of tailors, seamstresses and scraps of leftover fabric to make dolls clothes, I was in my own mini paradise. I would design dresses for my dolls and do fashion shows and dream of becoming a fashion designer one day. I knew exactly what I wanted to do when I grew up, and in a round about sort of way, I made it. It was going to be either fashion or playing the piano. I have a gift for playing the piano by ear. We did not even own a piano but I knew I could play, and every time we went to visit someone who had a piano, I would beg to be allowed to play. I would think of a tune, place my hands on the keys and play it, chords and all. At the age of five – my parents and their friends were astounded. I didn't know what all the fuss was about as I thought everyone could do this – like writing, or drawing. The closest thing we had to a piano was a harmonium with a small, two octave keyboard powered by bellows. You pumped with one hand and played with the other. Which was terribly tedious, as I wanted to use both hands. So, my poor Ayah had to pump the bellows while I played. You can picture this spoilt child, can't you!

My parents finally tracked down a piano, which was being sold by an English couple who were going back home. I remember the feverish excitement when it arrived and was carried up the large flight of stairs with great care. It was a beauty and I played to my heart's content. My sister Feroza was already having piano lessons at the time, so Mum thought I should start as well. There was only one piano teacher in our town and as such, she was terribly snooty and very strict in her methods. Playing anything by ear was akin to devil worship. She tried in vain to stop me playing my favourite pop songs instead of practicing my scales the moment she left the room. She would return with a ruler and smack my knuckles. After 6 months of misery and very sore knuckles, my Mum said 'You can play perfectly well without lessons' so the horrid lessons stopped. The result was, of course, that I cannot read music and did not pursue a career as a pianist, but having the ability to reproduce any tune after hearing it just once, proved very useful when, many years later, I played all the music for Scout Group shows and performed in various concerts. When our younger son Jamsheed began showing the same gift, we made sure he had the best music teachers at school and finally Sussex University where he graduated, and is now a hugely successful pianist and singer. We were in England by then, so the choice of good training was vast!

When I was eleven, Dad was transferred to Nagpur with his job for the Life Insurance Corporation of India. So the whole family went to live in Nagpur, which is the geographical centre of India and one of the hottest regions. The temperature was regularly around 30-40 degrees (centigrade). Air conditioners would not work very well in that dry heat, so most houses had air coolers. These were large metal frames on stands, surrounded with a special kind of straw, which was kept constantly moist by circulating water. On a shelf in the middle was a huge exhaust fan, which blew the cooled air into the room. It had a lovely natural, grassy smell and worked a treat. The gardens had enormous bushes of poinsettias, bright red in the blazing sunshine.

I went to St. Joseph's Convent School and enjoyed making new friends. We had elocution lessons where we learned the art of debate and also social studies, which included politics and economics. We had to clasp our hands in front of us as we delivered our speeches. Drama was fun, too. I played the convict in 'The Bishop's Candlesticks' wearing a pair of striped pyjamas, with dirt on my face and my curly hair all frizzed up. My parents were in the audience and claimed they didn't recognise me. There was a piano in the Nagpur house as well. I realise now that my parents must have hired it especially because, in India, pianos were very rare objects in those days. Such love. Just before my final year of school, my Dad was transferred back to Poona, so, instead of disrupting my education too much, they decided to send me to boarding school for one year. This would be a sort of 'finishing school' as it was a lovely place high up in the Nilgiri Hills in South India. It was the Presentation Convent in Kodaikanal, in South India. This school was one of the best in all of India and operated by the Presentation order of nuns whose headquarters were in Matlock, Derbyshire. The English schools worked on a 'Senior Cambridge Certificate' system, which meant that the year went from

January to December, rather than September to June.

This was a wonderful year and I made even more new friends and discovered that nuns were fun people. Each morning we would be woken by Sister Mary Magdalene, bursting into the dormitory, reciting the 'Hail Mary', wearing a long white nightgown buttoned to the neck and long red hair down to her waist. That was the first revelation. Nuns had hair! Then we discovered her operatic voice and her ability to play the guitar. There were plenty of Irish nuns and on St. Patrick's Day (17th March) the girls would get up early, get dressed and serenade the nuns with Irish songs. For good measure we would do the same for the Scottish nuns (on St Andrew's Day, of course), and it goes without saying, 'Jerusalem' on St. Georges Day for the English nuns. There were no Welsh nuns, so St. David's day fell by the wayside. There were midnight feasts and an outing to the town every Saturday morning to spend our pocket money. The big treat was to visit the milk bar in town and have enormous milkshakes made with rich buffalo milk. We were certainly well fed. The first time we were served bananas after tea, I proceeded to peel it and as I bit into it, was swiftly admonished by the nun on duty – 'Is that how you eat a banana? Only monkeys eat bananas like that. Peel it, put it on your plate and eat it with a knife and fork.' So I did. To this day I'm not sure if she was setting me up.

Being away from the family for a whole year, aged thirteen, was a scary idea as was the prospect of rubbing shoulders with daughters of diplomats, maharajas and nobility. My mother gave me a good pep talk before I left on the train for Kodai – 'Just be yourself, have confidence in everything you do, stand up for yourself, be nice to people and if all else fails, play the piano – not everyone can do that!' It worked. I was the youngest in my class and had no business sitting for a final school-leaving exam at the age of fourteen, but that's the way it worked out. There was another girl at PCK who played the piano by ear. Her name was Janet Hunt. One morning we surprised the whole school by playing two pianos together for assembly – 'Teddy Bears Picnic' it was.

That summer the nuns took our entire year to Kashmir for a two-week holiday. Bearing in mind that Kashmir is in the far north of India and we were in the far south, it was a long journey by train and coach. I did not know much about my mother's journey many years earlier at that time. We went by air-conditioned train from Madras (now Chenai) to New Delhi, and then by coach to Pathankot and up to Srinagar where we stayed on houseboats on the lake. There were avenues of poplars and walnut trees on the way and the traders would come to our houseboat with their 'shop boat' full of goodies like walnut chocolates and fresh red apples. We visited fantastic woollen mills where they wove exquisite stoles and then hand embroidered them. We went to colourful carpet workshops and also saw craftspeople making intricate wood carvings and papier maché boxes, which were intricately decorated in beautiful jewel colours.

It was such a great privilege to have visited Srinagar. At that time it was relatively peaceful in Kashmir, the jewel of India. It is one of the many trouble spots in the world, now. Why can't some people realize how precious little time we have on this beautiful planet and make better use of it, rather than fighting over something that accomplishes nothing. What a feat it must have been to take twenty five 14 – 16 year old girls on such an expedition, and what a great responsibility.

On the way back, the coach stopped at Pahlgam, before beginning the descent towards Delhi. We were told to remain in the coach while the nuns went into the coach station to make some enquiries. I remember looking at the low wall outside and seeing it move up and down but thought nothing of it – perhaps it was us shifting around in the coach. We were told nothing, but apparently there had been a severe earth tremor and the road ahead had been blocked by a rockslide. By the time we reached Delhi – completely unaware of the situation – there were telegrams all the way from England and America, major panic and relief at finding us all safe and sound. The nuns in charge must have been worried sick, but the joys of youth could not see what all the fuss was about. It was quite an adventure with lots of happy memories.

After I returned from Kodaikanal we were not sure how well I had fared in my SCC exams so, on the safe side, I was enrolled into yet another school – St Anne's Convent school in Poona where my aunt Zenobia was a PE teacher. (Very proud of her name, she once paid for the entire family to go to the cinema to see a film of the same name, thinking it must be about some beautiful princess. Zenobia, however, turned out to be an elephant).

This meant that I had to prepare for the Senior School Certificate exam (Indian system) the following June. So I had to cram all the stuff they had been learning, including two new subjects and another Shakespeare play and a whole lot of complicated maths into less than six months. I did it - and, what's more, I passed both the SCC and the SSC with flying colours at the tender age of fourteen going on fifteen. Needless to say, I don't remember much of what I crammed into my brain for the exams, but it has been very useful for Trivia challenges and crossword puzzles.

Chapter 5: Out for a Fling and Ring-a-ding ding

After all this, I started at Wadia College in Poona to get my BA degree, which was a three-year course. The college formed part of Poona University and as it was very near to our house, I could walk or cycle there easily. Those years were supremely happy too. Quite apart from studying for a degree in English Language and Literature and Educational Philosophy and Psychology, I met Jehan, who was to be the love of my life for many, many years to come.

In 1964, his family had just arrived to live in Poona from Dar-es-Salaam in East Africa where his father had established a highly successful law firm. The British had left Tanganyika (now Tanzania) and it seemed a good time to leave, too. Jehan was born in Bombay on 16th Oct. 1945 and when he was very little the family moved to New Delhi for a while, where his father, Kaikushroo Master, was legal advisor to Jawaharlal Nehru during the granting of Independence to India by the British. They lived in a house next door to where the great Mahatma Gandhi was assassinated while delivering one of his daily sermons on peace and non-violent protest. On the 30th of January 1948, Jehan remembers hearing three gun shots and being scooped up in the garden and rushed indoors by Joseph, their long serving retainer who did everything, from cooking to looking after the children.

Jehan's Mum & Dad Amy & Keki
in Dar-es-salaam

When Jehan's father's work with Nehru
was done, the family emigrated to Dar-es-
Salaam. Life was good, the law firm flourished
and his Dad became a highly respected judge
(having himself graduated from Edinburgh
University and London in the company of Lord
Denning with whom he maintained contact for
many, many years). Jehan's older sister Meher
also went into law – which ensured that Jehan
would never follow that profession however
lucrative it may prove to be. Two lawyers in one
family was quite enough argument.

He went to school in Dar and when he
was nine, his parents thought it would be fitting to
send him to boarding school in England. Well,
this must have been terrifying.

There were no direct flights in those days, and the plane made several stops along the way. He was under the eye of the airline staff and travelled all by himself to an unfamiliar country, to be met at London Airport by a representative of Sharrow School for Boys in Haywards Heath, Sussex. I suppose one called it 'character building' and that it certainly was. The rules at the school were ridiculously strict and 'Tom Brown's School days' comes to mind. He stuck it out for a year, being thoroughly homesick and trying very hard to enjoy the cold early morning PE sessions. Joining the Scouts, which was part of the school curriculum, seems to have been the high spot for him as it brought back the free open-air lifestyle he would have grown up with in East Africa.

Happily, his parents soon decided this was not for him, and repatriated him to Dar where he finished his schooling while spending hours on the beach, fishing and camping out overnight, learning to drive the family car at the age of twelve and loving every minute. His driving skills were put into action one day when, at fourteen years of age, he was visiting a relative who was on a Sisal plantation in the middle of nowhere. Rusi, his cousin, had an altercation with some machinery and accidentally chopped off his finger. Bleeding profusely, he calmly ordered Jehan to take the car keys and drive him to the nearest hospital in Kilosa, which was some twenty-five miles away. Rusi bravely held on to his finger and somehow managed to stay alive.

However, the surgeons did not manage to attach the finger back on.

Jehan's parents' large and beautiful home was built facing the sea and must have been fantastic, with the spectacular African sunrise over the sea every single day. His parents had a wonderful life, with parties and safaris. His mother was a Commissioner for the Girl Guides and a friend of Lady Baden Powell.

'Ocean View' Jehan's home in Dar

Towards the end of Jehan's school years, his father decided it was time to retire and go back to India, as East Africa had gained Independence from British rule and times were changing. Fortuitously, their choice of town was Poona and Jehan was enrolled into Wadia College. To begin with, he had to live in the college hostels while his parents sorted out the grand move back to India and found a house to rent. He promptly made lots of new friends, most of whom were quite disreputable. He had a jolly time learning how to smoke, drink and ride motorbikes – or maybe he was *teaching* the others! Anyway, he was most popular and having a ball.

His parents finally settled into their new home. One morning, my mother was driving home after a game of tennis, when she stopped to give a lift to Dhun Mehta, who had a reputation for being slightly eccentric and was also the village telegraph. She was actually rather sweet but looked most peculiar because she was very short, very thin, had a wizened face and deep, sunken eyes and always wore her sari up to her ankles with thick black boots. She walked everywhere, with her long black umbrella tucked under her arm and looking like the wicked witch of the west.

She was as fit as a fiddle, which is more than you can say about the average Parsi lady in Poona at the time. She also played tennis in her sari and was most disapproving of my mother and her friends, who wore short white tennis skirts. What a character. Anyway – she climbed into the car and said she was on her way to meet some relatives who had just arrived from East Africa and it would be lovely to introduce them to my parents, so that they could get to make some new friends. That is how my mum met Jehan's mum Amy, who was pretty, charming and a beautician, and was also planning to start her own business from home.

Needless to say, they got on famously and during the course of the conversation Amy said, 'I'm not so happy about the company my son is keeping – I would like him to meet a better class of young people. So, my Mum promptly invited him to Feroza's 21st Birthday Party the following week, where he could perhaps meet this 'better class of people'. Reluctantly, he came – this new 'England returned' boy with a posh accent. Being a rebel at heart, he was not going to be impressed by high society, having been steered towards it all his life. When the girl he was dancing with dropped her contact lens, (which were quite a modern thing at that time), we all started to look for it on the black and white marble floor. There was this imperious 'Whose fat foot is that – move it!' The voice was his and the foot was mine. That is how we met. I thought he was very rude and I smirked when he discovered the contact lens in the cuff of his trousers. He didn't stay for the entire evening and disappeared to meet his disreputable gang of friends.

The next day I saw him at college. Being four years younger made a lot of difference then and I was the innocent, naïve student who was there to gain knowledge and a degree. I also had a gentle, quiet boyfriend of sorts – uninteresting but very kind. In short, rather boring. I don't know quite how it came about, but one fine day, Jehan asked if I would like to go on a motorbike ride.

Whether it was a dare on the part of his gang or genuine besottedness, I never did find out. It sounded exciting, a trifle dangerous and I would also be cutting a class. I accepted. Off we went (remember, no helmets and me sitting side-saddle on the back holding on for dear life). A few miles out of town we saw, coming towards us in her trusty black Morris Oxford, my old PE mistress, of whom I had always been terrified. Knowing that her first port of call would be to my mother to tell her where her trusted daughter was, I ducked, hoping she hadn't seen me. She had, and she did.

We carried on regardless up a hill, and stopped. Sitting on a rock looking out over the urban sprawl that was Poona, he put his arm around my shoulders and said, 'Now, don't get the wrong idea, because I'm only out for a fling.' Not being at all sure what a fling was but it felt quite nice, I said 'Me, too'. Well, that was over 50 years ago as I write this.

Later that evening when I got home from college Mum said 'Had a good day?' and I said 'Yes' and she said 'Do anything special?' To which I said 'Did you get a 'phone call?' fully expecting a long lecture on trust and good upbringing. To my surprise, she was highly amused and probably quite relieved to find I had it in me to occasionally do something wild. All she said was 'I'm glad you were with that nice boy'. Well, there was no answer to that. He had obviously charmed his future mother-in-law completely.

After that, we had great times in college, organising variety shows, taking part in debates and even setting up a student union of sorts. This came about because motorbikes were being ridden at great speed around the college campus and the Principal ordered barriers, in the form of long ladders, to be placed across the roads. We objected, on the grounds that the girls could not step over them in their tight skirts without indecent exposure. Especially, short, tight skirts. Unbelievably, this fired the imagination of several students and also the local press. There were placards and posters and it caused so much chaos that the ladders were finally removed. All harmless fun. College days were happy days!

Our Professor for English Literature was a large, rotund lady who always wore a sari. This is a very forgiving garment and covers most sins. However, halfway through the lesson, as she teetered to and fro on the edge of the teacher's platform, her bra would become uncomfortable. So, during the course of her lecture, thinking that nobody would notice as the sari would cover her tracks, she would discreetly unhook it from behind. Well, it was like the sinking of the Titanic. She did this every single time, so we soon started taking bets on the exact time the event would take place. It's quite astounding that we actually passed our exams with flying colours – me with a BA in English Language and Literature and Philosophy and Psychology of Education (after which I became a dress designer...) and Jehan with a BA in Politics, Philosophy and Economics, followed by an MBS in Business studies (after which he became a computer programmer).

I also passed my driving test. In spite of the fact that driving anywhere in India was a nightmare, the test itself was held within the confines of the compound (lovely old-fashioned word, that) of the Driving Licence Authority building. It involved reversing into a parking space marked out by four sticks, driving round the perimeter without stalling the engine and answering a few inane questions about traffic lights – which, in reality, not many drivers took any notice of. There was no other vehicle in the vicinity of your driving test. So, if you failed that, there was something seriously wrong. Things must be quite different now, though the cows still have right of way, wherever. They are a natural traffic-calmer and much prettier than speed humps.

All I wanted to do was to make clothes and design unusual dresses. When I was little, Barbie dolls had just been invented. I had one. She had her dresses changed every five minutes. As I mentioned earlier, the tailor made all our clothes, so I used to beg scraps of leftover fabric from him and turn them into all sorts of exotic garments. During recess times in school I would have a bevy of girls round me as I sketched and designed their wedding dresses, in spite of the fact that most of us would wear a sari on our wedding day! Fashion magazines from England and the USA were like gold dust and would be passed from house to house and never thrown away.

The tailors made all the clothes without a pattern. Knowledge passed from father to son. Why were there no women tailors? I expect someone had to do the cooking, cleaning and housekeeping.

Also, there were no dressmaking classes, let alone a school of fashion. So, my wonderful parents came to the rescue. My father was a very keen Rotarian and had many friends all over the world thanks to Rotary International. There was a monthly magazine for Rotary with a Pen Friend page. My mother was a keen letter-writer and started corresponding with the wives of several Rotarians. The year Dad became Governor for Rotary, my parents made a grand tour of the USA and stayed with many different families, thanks to my mother having made so many friends. She used to exchange Christmas gifts and correspond with them regularly, so by the time my parents met them, they were old mates. One of my mother's contacts was a lady named Rosemarie Eshbach, who lived in Reading, Pennsylvania. She was a designer, a dressmaker and a lecturer at Albright University in Reading. When she heard about my yearnings to learn fashion design, she promptly suggested, nay, insisted, that I come to live with her family for a year and she would teach me all I needed to know, with hands-on experience.

This was an offer they could not refuse. Rosemarie and Ken, who owned a successful building construction company, had four children, including a girl the same age as me. As soon as I graduated with my degree, it was with great excitement that I set off, with my mother, to see the rest of the world.

Chapter 6: Spreading my Wings

My sister had married an Italian in 1965 and lived in Milan, with a beautiful house on Lake Como. This came about because she went to Italy on a student exchange programme called 'An Experiment in International Living'. Having spent three weeks living with an Italian family and loving every minute, she returned to India with her head in a spin. A few days later, she took Dad along for a walk and said "I've met this wonderful Italian boy called Andrea, and he wants to marry me." So Dad took a deep breath and said, "Do you love him?" to which she replied in the affirmative, of course. They then had a discussion with Mum, who said, simply, "If he loves you truly, he must come to India and ask for your hand in marriage. That way, we can get to know him and make sure he is going to make you happy."

So, my mother started corresponding with Andrea's mother and thought about having Italian lessons. Andrea arrived the following month, by which time the Registrar had been booked for a wedding ceremony at home, followed by a huge reception at the Royal Western India Turf Club. I don't think my parents had any intention of refusing permission! Everything felt right. We all fell in love with Andrea – he spoke a reasonable amount of English, confusing 'chicken' with 'kitchen', and was absolutely charming.

Feroza and Andrea's house on lake Como

My parents did not know then that his family owned a flourishing paper mill in Milan and had several properties on Lake Como. They married, and Feroza went to live in Italy. Nine months later she gave birth to twin boys – Roberto and Francesco. A year later, Davide was born. There are now six grandchildren (all girls) and still counting. I cannot imagine the thoughts that went through our parents' heads as they considered sending their first born to live on the other side of the world. They went out to see her soon after and were very satisfied that they had made the right decision, but the moment they returned from Italy, my mother said to me – "If you're planning to go and meet her, you'd better learn Italian, because nobody speaks English there." And why should they? So, she set about finding us an Italian tutor.

There was only one Italian in Poona. He was the Managing Director of the hugely successful Vespa factory, which made the thousands of two-wheeler scooters that clogged the streets of India. As such, he was a Very Important Person. This did not stop my Mum from ringing up the Vespa factory and asking to speak to him. She explained the situation and, to our delight, he absolutely insisted on coming over every evening to give us lessons in conversational Italian and refused any payment as he said it would be a joy to be able to speak Italian with us! The first lesson consisted of his warning me about Italian gigolos, who might follow me around murmuring sweet nothings. I was to turn around and say, in the strictest voice possible, 'Cosa voi?' (what do you want?), followed by 'Vai via!' (Go away). Once he was confident that I had mastered this technique, we continued with our lessons and I looked forward to meeting these handsome Italian gigolos.

The visit to the USA began with my mother and me going to see Feroza and Andrea and their three lovely little boys at Lake Como. Our knowledge of Italian came in very useful as neither of her in-laws spoke any English. Lake Como is one of the most beautiful places on earth, and the view from their house is stupendous. The garden slopes down to the boathouse on the lake. All along the edge of the garden are olive trees, from which they make their own olive oil each year. The garden is stupendous, with kiwifruits, kumquats and lemons growing happily outdoors alongside the camellias and hydrangeas.

As an unusual interlude, we then flew to the Isle of Man to visit one of my cousins, another intrepid young lady who had married a delightful Englishman and ran a hotel in Ramsay. This was quite an experience, as we had never before had the dubious pleasure of enjoying four British seasons in one day. The wind howled, the rain lashed and then the sun came out. We spent a few days with them. My mother then stayed on with my cousin and I continued on my own to New York. Let the adventure begin.

I flew from Douglas, in the Isle of Man, to London Heathrow, and needed to change terminals for my flight to New York. I had been given all the lectures about strange men, not so strange men and talking to strangers in general. I was eighteen, bright-eyed, very bushy-tailed and clueless in the wicked ways of the world. When a polite young porter saw me struggling with my suitcases at Heathrow's Terminal 1 and said "Hello, Darlin', can I 'elp you with your bags?" I panicked slightly because any strange man calling you 'Darlin' was to be treated with caution. I had no choice but to hand over my bags and he very kindly escorted me to Terminal 2, which was the International terminal, as there were only two at the time. "There you are, love" he said, smiled and turned on his heels. It was terribly exciting, and me wearing a bright orange and green silk sari, so that the Eshbachs would recognize me when I arrived in New York.

This was a wonderful family. Little Greg stared at me in awe as he had never seen an Indian who didn't wear feathers and face paint. As we walked towards their enormous Cadillac, he said "This is a CAR. Have you seen a car before?" and I replied that indeed, I had, and could also drive one, as elephants were out of fashion now. Not to be outdone, he said, "We have a SWIMMING POOL. Do you know what a swimming pool is?" and I explained that India was full of swimming pools because it was always hot. We stopped at a service station on the way, so I asked if we were stopping for petrol. "What's petrol, Mum?" The reply came "Gas, honey, gas." I had my first BLT (Bacon, lettuce and to-may-to) sandwich, American style, on the way to Reading, Pennsylvania.

The Eshbachs looked after me as if I was their own daughter, and I had the time of my life. Rosemarie took me to factory outlets for fabrics and to various design studios, taught me pattern making and all sorts of clever techniques to simplify dressmaking. To top it all, she had a magnificent piano, which I could play to my heart's content. She was a very good cook and while she was as slim as any fashion model, I promptly put on about 40 lbs in weight – no kidding. We had milk with every meal, ice-cream, maple syrup, huge steaks and mayonnaise. I ate exactly the same as the other children but did half the exercise. At one barbecue they took me to, I was given such a large serving of steak that I thought it was to be shared with the entire table. On weekends there were family picnics in the stunning Pennsylvanian countryside. They took me to Pittsburg and Gettysburg and I could kick myself for not paying enough attention to American history while I was there, but I was too busy having a grand time.

Towards the end of my stay with the Eshbach family, I went to spend a month with Elsa and Charlie Powers in Boston. They were also friends of my parents through Rotary and when he had visited, my Dad gave a talk at the Boston Rotary Club, which seemed to have impressed them thoroughly. The Powers family had four sons. Hmmm. I was a very special addition and was soon called 'Charlie's girl'. He owned a hugely successful Insurance Company (the same business as my Dad) in downtown Boston, and one day he took me in to work with him. I was requested to wear a sari. In those days this was an unusual sight and very much admired and appreciated. The fact that I wore an exotic costume, looked thoroughly foreign but spoke better English than most people around me was a source of great interest. After the first few days the novelty wore off and I turned up wearing a dress and worked part time at the office, typing notes and making the tea. In my lunch hour I would join the others for a sandwich (half a loaf of bread and three tins of tuna mayonnaise) aboard one of the boats moored in the harbour.

Charlie and his girl in Boston

Boston is a beautiful city, steeped in American history, so one afternoon my friend Betty and I decided we would take a walk round the 'Freedom Trail', which was a series of yellow footprints that led you from one historical monument to another. One of these was a statue of Benjamin Franklin. On the way there, we saw a group of Indians, the ladies all wearing bright and colourful saris. Without warning Betty, I walked up to one of these ladies and, putting on my finest American accent, I said, admiringly, "Gee, is that a sa-ree? Isn't it something!" The lady, all smiles and truly delighted, explained to me at great length, that the sari was 6 yards long (no pun intended), and she all but took it off to give me a demonstration of how to wear it. After oohing and aahing while Betty looked on, totally bemused, I asked the lady where she was from. When she said "Bombay" I dropped the accent and said "I'm from Poona." Her face was a treat. Still, they had a good laugh. We carried on to the Franklin monument and saw an elderly couple sitting on the steps. As we stopped to take photos, the man beckoned me over and said "I'm a Psychic. I feel I have to tell you something." Curious as ever, we sat down to listen. He made a trance like face and said "I can see you wearing a long costume and standing in front of the Taj Mahal, perhaps you are wearing a sari." I gasped. Then he continued – "Are you from a town beginning with P?" Sharp intake of breath. After he had impressed me completely with his psychic powers, he let on that he had overheard my antics with the Indian party and thought I should have a taste of my own medicine!

The Powers had a holiday home in Hyannisport, on Cape Cod. Elsa was also a friend of Rose Kennedy, the mother of the great John Fitzgerald Kennedy. Elsa asked me if I would like her to arrange for us to go to tea at the Kennedy mansion. I am ashamed to say that I probably did not show enough enthusiasm, as I was eighteen and there were more interesting things going on, so she let it drop, as it would have been a hugely complicated security procedure to arrange a visit. I did, however, see young Caroline and brother John-John playing on the post office steps in Hyannisport one morning. What a tragic history that family has had.

Elsa was also an accomplished dressmaker and taught me even more skills and tricks of the trade. Several of her relations had houses on Cape Cod. One of her brothers lived by the lake. They organised a lobster party one night, so Elsa took me along to buy the lobsters. We went to an extensive lobster farm and she chose ten giant specimens from the tanks. She asked the salesman to prepare them and put them in the car. After wandering about for a bit, we set off home with the large brown paper bags containing the lobsters in the footwell of the back seat. I kept hearing rustling sounds and thought it was my imagination, but as they got louder I mentioned it to Elsa who calmly said "I expect it's the lobsters trying to get out' – at which I shrieked, 'They're alive?" She then explained "Of course, we have to drop them in boiling water to cook them just before we eat them." Well, I didn't know that, and kept glancing nervously at the back seat wondering whether I should try and set them free before this terrible fate overtook them. However, we did cook them that evening, dipped them in butter, wore large plastic bibs and ate them. They were unbelievably delicious.

While still with the Powers family, I went with them to Vermont where one of their sons was at University. It was late September and the autumn colours were stunning. Every shade of red, yellow, gold, and umpteen variations of green mixed in. No matter what, Nature always wins first prize for an artistic display! It was such a privilege to be here at just the right time.

Following my adventures with the Powers I returned to Rosemarie and saw my first ever snowfall in October. The golden autumn leaves were still on the trees as the snow was unexpectedly early. It was utterly beautiful and I was thrilled, as I had only ever seen snow in pictures and on Christmas cards. (Yes, we had Indian Christmas cards with pictures of snow)....don't ask.

Soon, it was time for me to go back to India and Rosemarie had arranged for me to visit her niece Judy, also a fashion designer, who lived in Brooklyn and worked in Manhattan, New York. So I went to spend a week with her, just before I was due to fly out. She and her husband lived in a typical Brooklyn house – basement, wide stone steps up to the front door, with an imposing staircase which was a bit grim until you reached their flat, which was lovely. I visited Judy's studio in Manhattan, where she designed and made up the patterns, which were then put together by sample machinists before they went into major production. I also got to explore New York. Before the week was out, I received a 'phone call from my cousin Rashna, who was in New York, very homesick and staying with some friends in Long Island. She absolutely insisted that I should postpone my flight to India and spend a few days with her, as she 'just had to see someone from home.'

So, we arranged to meet at Macy's department store in Manhattan. It was HUGE. I had rung my parents earlier and told them that I would be delaying my flight, not thinking for an instant about the panic I must have caused. Not that they could have done much about it, anyway. I went to stay with my cousin's friends, Bob and Audrey Mullaney, in Long Island, who made me very welcome. Rashna had known them only a short time herself, and here they were, putting the two of us up just out of friendship and generosity. Bizarre, yes, but what good people there are in the world. We forget that there are many more good people than bad – they just don't write about them in the papers. By that time, I was running out of money, so, with great confidence, cousin Rashna said, "I'll get us a job."

She walked into a Ski Shop, which also made fur coats (in Fifth Avenue, no less). It was called André Ski and was owned by Monsieur André, who was a fur coat couturier of high repute. Rashna described my qualifications as 'expert designer and couturier' and we got ourselves a job. There were several Latin-American employees of highly questionable legal origin in the workshop, all female and very skilled. I knew absolutely nothing about fur coats. So began my foray into the world of high fur fashion.

Mr. André had some very special customers. Among them were Sophia Loren, Jaqueline (Kennedy) Onassis and a few other jaw-dropping names. Mr. André was a delightful man of slight stature with a white goatee beard. He realised quite early on that I was genuinely interested in learning more about the process of manufacturing fur coats than simply machining bits of lining together.

One day, he took me into his pattern cutting room and said he would show me how to cut out a fur coat. Stretched out on the huge cutting table was a real leopard skin, right side down. As the pattern was already drawn on it in chalk, I was handed a scalpel and taught how to hold it at an angle to cut through the skin in a way that, when the pieces were sewn together, the fur would overlap and conceal the seam. I was allowed to cut out the pieces for the hat that went with this wonderful coat, which was, so he told me, being made for Sophia Loren. Looking back on it now, I cannot believe that people hunted these beautiful wild animals just for their skins and that I was not the slightest bit shocked at what I had been allowed to do. In fact, I was thrilled to bits.

The following week, someone called Jimi Hendrix was coming to the shop to have a fitting for a sheepskin coat lined in mink. The girls were feverish with excitement but were asked to be quiet, well behaved and out of sight during his visit. We were allowed to watch through a slit window in the workroom door. I (honestly) did not know who this Jimi Hendrix was, so I thought he must be some gorgeously good-looking actor or celebrity. The day dawned and at 11am, a sleek black limousine drew up outside the shop. Two elegant black men in shiny black suits and dark glasses got out. I thought, 'He's got to be one of them'. Then, this scruffy individual with lots of fuzzy hair, torn jeans and a gold medallion over an unbuttoned shirt, emerged and joined them. I thought 'He's probably the chap who carries the bags'. They all came into the shop. You could have heard a pin drop as the heat of excitement grew in the workroom. As we all crowded behind the door, hoping to get a glimpse of the great man, I asked the girl closest to me "Which one's Jimi Hendrix?" at which there was a communal shriek of disbelief and shock at my ignorance. I got us all into trouble and destroyed all credibility with the staff. But I did discover who Jimi Hendrix was and why he was so famous.

Each morning, my cousin and I would take the train from Long Island to Manhattan and cut through Central Park on the odd occasion. As nobody had told us about what usually happened to young girls in miniskirts, fishnet tights and long boots in Central Park, especially after dusk, nothing did ever happen, but writing to our parents and telling them about our adventures must have all but finished them off. One evening we faced one of New York's spectacular blizzards. We managed to get to our station on Long Island (I forget the name) from where it was a relatively short walk to the house - only half a mile. However, the snow was knee-deep and we were wearing the shortest miniskirts and next to useless fashion boots. Traffic was at a standstill, so Bob could not come to fetch us either. So we trudged home through the snow in this raging blizzard, in the dark, hanging on to each other. We were lucky nobody broke a leg – wouldn't have felt it, anyway!

After spending the week that turned into six in New York and having the time of my life, I finally boarded a flight back to Milan. During my short stay with Feroza and Andrea, they took me to the Opera at La Scala, to see *La Bohème,* because Andrea had heard that a young tenor called Placido Domingo was giving his debut performance. This was a rare treat and totally unforgettable.

When I returned to India, my parents and Jehan came to fetch me at Bombay's Santa Cruz Airport and were aghast at seeing the size I was. Mum put me on a strict diet of boiled food and vegetables and within the year I was back to a tidy size 12. As there was plenty of space in my parents' huge house, I set up the first ready-made dress boutique in Poona.

I designed, bought beautiful fabrics and sewed. I would do all the cutting and we employed a tailor to put things together, after which I hand finished each garment. Business was brilliant, as this was something new and exciting for the girls at college and their mothers. My mother enjoyed it too, and I used Mary Quant as my inspiration, with lots of black and white and psychedelic prints. Can-can skirts were out and miniskirts, cutaway shoulders, shifts and hipster bell bottom trousers were in, and the brighter, the better. Fun. My Dad named it 'Boutique Eleganza' after he got over the shock of seeing the first mini (16"), and asking if it was a skirt or a loincloth. I would set up little fashion shows, getting my friends to model – instead of dressing my dolls, as I used to, I was dressing real people! As word got around, I began getting commissions to design special occasion outfits and this kept me really busy.

Soon after I set up this little business, Jehan and two of his friends (both named Daraius), set off on their voyage of discovery to the Middle East and Europe. We were separated for another year but it did not make the slightest difference to our being joined at the hip.

'Boutique Eleganza'   Poona 1969

Chapter 7: Jehan's Voyage of Discovery

Jehan's adventures were much more colourful than mine. The three of them had heard that in Kuwait, the wealthy Sheikhs abandoned their expensive cars by the wayside when they got bored with them and the cars were there for the taking. So they thought, naively, they would go to Kuwait, help themselves to one of these free vehicles, and drive across the Middle East to Europe. Well, abandoned cars there certainly were, but you were not allowed to take them out of the country!

Jehan flew to Kuwait with the intention of finding this luxurious car and the other two went by cargo boat to Basra, in Iraq, armed with the 'phone number of a friend of a friend. The 'phone number did not exist, so they checked into a hotel to await Jehan's arrival. He arrived by bus and tried the same number – no luck – so he also checked into a hotel, wondering what to do next. Mercifully, it turned out to be the same hotel, so they were reunited. (No mobile 'phones, remember). Car-less, they decided to hitchhike all the way to Europe. On arriving at the Syrian border, they were in for a shock. Jehan had a British passport, and as the Syrian guards had not seen one of these for a very long time, they stuck a rifle in his back and locked him up. After many explanations, they agreed to give the boys a military escort to the Turkish border. The boys climbed into an army truck and surrounded by heavily armed but friendly soldiers, they arrived in Turkey. They then took a bus to Ankara. Jehan was a pipe smoker at the time and a Turkish stranger on the bus gave him a large bag of tobacco as a gift. This he accepted with gratitude and a great deal of suspicion, sniffing it carefully just to make sure!

They arrived in Istanbul, and were overwhelmed by the sights and sounds of this amazing city, which is at the junction of two great continents, and steeped in history. They must have looked very dirty and bedraggled, because a very kind Muslim gentleman, who was convinced that they must be Muslim, invited them to the Turkish Baths, where they were steamed, pumelled and scrubbed, and then took them to the local Mosque to say their prayers. Too grateful to put the man right, they duly went, and were cleansed of all their sins. They then decided to stay at the local YMCA, and spent the next few days taking in the beauty of Istanbul – the Topkapi Palace with all its jewels, the Sultan Ahmed (Blue) Mosque and the Hagia Sofia, which was over the years, a church and a mosque, but is now a beautiful museum.

As Bulgaria and Yugoslavia were then Communist countries, hitch-hiking was prohibited, so they found themselves on a train from the Turkish border to Trieste, in Italy, from where they would go to Feroza's in Milan, buy a little Fiat cinquecento and drive to England. As they settled into their train compartment, a rather large Bulgarian lady got in, struggling with a bulging suitcase and another, very heavy box with a handle. They helped her install her luggage and she gave them a wide smile, all gaps and gold teeth. They smiled back and nodded and shrugged and made the sort of wordless conversation one has when language is a major barrier. So the journey continued. At the station just before they arrived at the Italian border, some heavily armed customs guards boarded the train. The lady's attitude suddenly changed, and, with a very alarmed expression, she pointed to the box under the seat and indicated that, should the guards question it, the boys should say that it was theirs, not hers. Before they could question the wisdom of this, the guards had escorted her off the train after asking her to open her suitcase, which revealed all sorts of watches, jewellery and other clandestine goods, which she was clearly trying to smuggle into Italy. The box, however, was missed and remained on the train.

After they were safely across the border and all was quiet, they decided to take a look inside. The mystery object that had caused such a panic was a sewing machine. A heavy, industrial Russian made Naumann sewing machine. So, rather than simply abandon it on the train, they lugged it over to my sister's house in Milan. Three young hitchhikers and a sewing machine (good title for a book). She bought it off them for the equivalent of £25 and with that money, they bought a rusty old Fiat cinquecento with very dodgy brakes. In this wonderful iconic car they set off on the Grand European Discovery. Their journey took them through Switzerland into Germany. They camped along the way and got work as bricklayers and road workers to earn a crust. There is a stretch of pavement outside a famous department store in Dusseldorf, which bears their stamp.

On the way to Dusseldorf, the trusty Fiat broke down, or rather, a part fell out. They found themselves in a little village with not a garage or a hotel in sight. So, deciding it was too late in the day to worry about it, they slept in the car. (Anyone who has sat in a Fiat 500 will realize that this was a feat for three large lads). However, the next morning a couple from one of the houses came over and invited them in to wash and have some breakfast. When they explained their story and the situation with the car, their kind host drove them to a garage, bought the required part at his expense, and helped them repair the car. Such acts of kindness would be rare these days, considering how rough they must have looked!

So they continued through Germany, into France and the port of Calais. They boarded a ferry to Dover and drove to Wimbledon where they stayed with friends. The other two flew back to Bombay a few days later but Jehan stayed on as he intended to settle in England. While sending out job applications he started work at `Bentalls ' in Kingston-upon-Thames. The store is still here many years later but completely changed.

Meanwhile, both sets of parents were busy arranging a wedding in Poona. Right through our years apart, we wrote to each other every single week. Computers and emails did not exist then, so it would take several days for letters to arrive. The date for the wedding was set at 15th February 1970 and Jehan flew back a week earlier. It was so wonderful to have him back!

Our wedding was held in the garden of my parents' house. A small stage was set up for the ceremony, decorated with garlands of flowers – roses, jasmine and marigolds – the scent was everywhere. My wedding sari was white, with broderie anglaise and Jehan wore a white dugli (a high collared cotton coat with white trousers). There is an amusing ritual at the beginning of a Parsi wedding ceremony where the couple sit facing each other, holding, in their right fists, a handful of grains of rice - (raw, in case you're wondering). A very long piece of string, symbolically to bind us together, is wound round both the chairs. A thin muslin curtain is held between us so that we cannot see each other. When the curtain is dropped, we are both supposed to throw the rice at each other, and the partner who throws first is, traditionally, the bossy one. Well, I flung my rice with gusto, but nobody had told Jehan what he was supposed to do with this rice, so he meekly let it drop to the floor. Of course, there is no truth in this tradition. We all know who the boss in this household is. Then, after everyone had a good laugh, the two priests made sure of our union with lengthy prayers, accompanied with throwing of more rice and rose petals.

At the end, we received blessings from all our parents in turn, lots of presents from all the guests – while all the time holding a coconut in our hands (good luck and fertility). We spent most of the time gazing into each other's eyes waiting for the night.

Long tables were set out under the trees for lunch, which was served on banana leaves instead of plates. It saved on the washing up and was totally ecological. It was a lovely day. February is a traditional month for weddings in India as the weather is usually reliably dry and not too hot. In the evening, the trees were lit up with hundreds of fairy lights and there was a huge reception, with plenty of dancing and alcohol. This was followed by yet another feast.

My sari for the evening was red silk woven with real gold thread. It was very heavy but beautiful. I forgot to mention that at each of these spectacular outdoor dinners and lunches, for which the catering is usually for between 200-500 people, the cooking is done on the premises. The Caterers bring their own kitchen and set it up in the garden, or wherever, and all is cooked from scratch. Impressive.

We flew to England a week later. The family came to Bombay to see us off and there were tearful farewells, although for the two of us it was an exciting adventure we were embarking upon. It was February in England, too. (Hmmm. Now, there's a surprise). There was also deep snow and it took a bit of getting used to. We went to stay with the same good friends in Wimbledon to start with. At that time, due to some bureaucratic Indian ruling, one was not allowed to take more than £100 out of India when one went abroad. So that is what we came to England with. Of course, £100 was worth a lot more then than it is now. Even so, we needed to get jobs and start earning some money. While Jehan was sending out his CVs and waiting for interviews, we worked for an East African importer of cotton clothing, and, equipped with the Morris Minor estate he lent us, we went around the South of England taking orders from fashion boutiques for these exotic *Kitange* shirts and dresses. It was terrific fun for not a lot of money, as it was commission-based. We got to know a lot of very pretty villages and some very nice pubs.

Meanwhile, I bought a secondhand sewing machine and did a bit of work for friends. A few weeks later, Jehan went for an interview with Lloyds Bank, which was being computerised. It was his first interview, and he landed a brilliant job as a computer operator, training on the job. When he first started with the bank, computers were huge machines, which were very noisy and took vast amounts of space. They also had key punch cards. By the time he retired, many years later, they were slim, lightweight and portable. Technology moves so fast, that by the time I finish writing this book there will be something we haven't even thought about right now.

As soon as we were able, we rented a small flat in Streatham, in southwest London. It cost us £4 a week and we shared a bathroom with the Irish couple upstairs. (Not at the same time, I hasten to add). Heating was courtesy of a paraffin heater, which threatened to burst into flames each time you lit it, and hot water was dependent on a gas meter, which had to be fed with shillings and was quite capable of running out while you were in the shower. The flat was truly grotty but we were in seventh heaven. I even acquired a piano, which was being discarded by a doctor at the local hospital. Thanks to a friend who was a nurse at the same hospital, this beautiful instrument in carved walnut wood was delivered to the flat in an ambulance! Health and Safety and NHS economies would never allow that now. I don't think it was actually allowed then, either.

However, with the help of two burly paramedics the patient was carried up the stairs and installed in the flat. Just don't tell anyone.

The weekly shop cost £5 in 1970. There was a little Sainsbury supermarket at the top of our road. It was more like a series of shops under one roof and very friendly. It did not take long to make friends wherever we were. Being brought up in India, I thought everyone spoke the Queen's English, so it came as a surprise to realize just how many regional accents there are. I once asked my Irish neighbour how she got her tea towels so white and she said "Bilem." So off I went to Sainsbury's to buy some 'Bilem'. Couldn't find any. When I asked her where she had got hers, she gave me a funny look and said "I just bile 'em, in a saucepan on the stove." The penny finally dropped.

From the outset, Jehan's job required him to work shifts. International banking involves having 24 hour contact with the rest of the world and dealing with various time zones. This meant working 8-hour shifts with 4 mornings, 4 afternoons and 4 nights followed by 4 days off to recuperate. We had plenty of time together. I also began taking a few dressmaking orders. My parents would come to visit every year and often stayed for three months at a time with us, and a month at my sister's in Italy. It was a bit of a squeeze in the little flat, but we managed. On one of her visits to Italy my mother brought the famous Naumann sewing machine for me from my sister, who decided it would make a fine wedding present! This must have been the machine's destiny. I used it for many, many years and it never let me down. The instructions were all in Russian so I never did work out all the tricks it did.

Never being content with making things to other people's ideas and designs, I started to design and make a collection of my own, but did not know how to go about selling it. A friend who held Tupperware parties suggested that I could hold Dress parties. She held the first one for me at her house. I took my collection along and took orders for making my designs to measure. This really took off, and soon I was holding several parties a month and working flat out, loving every minute. It turned into a very fine little business and I was being as creative as I dared. This was a great time for fashion and anything a bit risqué and outlandish was snapped up.

We spent two years in the flat in Streatham and then decided it was time to buy a house. With a mortgage from Lloyds Bank, we bought an end of terrace house in Edencourt Road, Streatham. As the flat had been let fully furnished, we had no furniture so, with his usual skill and enthusiasm Jehan set about making some. He made a fantastic pine bed with a design from the Reader's Digest DIY Manual, and a sturdy mahogany dining table frame with immaculate dovetail joints, for which we bought a huge piece of smoked glass from Pilkington's.

We actually saw the glass being manufactured at the factory, by special invitation. The bed and the table are still with us forty-five years later, with not a single creak or wobble.

This was the era of 'the good life' and I had a great ambition to have a vegetable garden. So we ripped up a perfectly good lawn and turned three-quarters of the garden into a potager. The neighbours must have been horrified. It was fairly successful, but infinitely cheaper and a darn sight easier to buy the veggies from the greengrocer! Yes, yes, I *know* that homegrown taste better, but that's probably psychological because it's jolly hard work.

Before we had the children, we had a dog. He arrived quite by accident. The same nurse friend who had organized our piano for us was given a Labrador cross puppy which had a brother who was going to be put down if nobody wanted him. What could we say? We went immediately to Hampstead to collect this black, hairy and totally cute puppy, which we named Scruffy for obvious reasons. His paws were far too big for the rest of him. His mother was a golden Labrador, but it appears an Irish wolfhound got through a large hole in the fence...so Scruffy had a beard as well. A more even-tempered dog I have yet to meet. He was affable, agreeable, affectionate, never barked and was totally untrainable. He chewed through our shoes, chewed through the furniture and ate anything and everything in sight. One day, somebody presented us with a three pound box of chocolates, all wrapped in cellophane with a big pink bow. We left the box on the sofa and went out for the evening. When we returned at midnight, a large black shape brushed past us into the garden and we entered the lounge to find the box open on the floor, with every single chocolate gone, except the mint one. Still, he survived in a haze of chocolate and we had him for seventeen years!

Jehan had some colleagues at the bank, who belonged to the Bromley and District Motor Club and asked us if we'd like to join. As this was exactly what he'd love to do, we did. The club held night rallies every month and we all took turns organizing them. Armed with detailed Ordnance Survey maps, compasses and roamers we set and followed trails in the Kent countryside, with clues to follow and marshalling points to arrive at. Health and Safety issues were a matter of common sense (what's that?) and the trickier the clues, the more the fun. Jehan was the Driver and I was his Navigator, with my magnifying lamp and map, shouting precise directions, like '20 yards sharp left' and he did exactly as he was told. Except that only once I shouted '20 yards sharp right' when it should have been 'sharp left' and we came to an abrupt but merciful halt between two perfectly placed trees on the edge of a cliff.

It was a bit like the movie 'The Italian Job' when the coach gets stuck with half of it hanging precariously off the edge. We had to crawl out of the rear windows very gingerly as the front wheels were in the air. The car was wedged between the trees. I love trees, as they can sometimes save your life. The Marshalls at the next checkpoint at the bottom of the hill could see a pair of driving headlights swinging up and down over the edge and it caused a major panic. Amazingly, the car survived as well as we did. It was a red Audi Super 90. We also owned a Land Rover with a winch at the time, as you do, so one of the others drove us home, we picked up the Land Rover, pulled the Audi to safety, and drove both cars home. No problem.

There were great times with the BDMC and we won several trophies and shields. Night rallies have been banned for years now. There just wasn't that much traffic on the roads in those days. Even so, I'm sure we must have been quite a nuisance, as we started at 11pm and finished in the early hours of the morning. There were powerful CIBIE driving lights on a detachable frame on the front of the car and Jehan removed them after each rally. One night, at around 3 am, we stopped in the main road to remove the lights before we got home, so as not to disturb the neighbours. A quiet police car came along and a burly officer got out. "Ello, 'ello, what's all this then?" He clearly thought we were in the process of nicking the lights off someone else's car. We explained and, most disbelievingly, he escorted us home and waited till we'd produced the house keys and gone inside. Nice to know they were on the job.

During the years before we started a family, we made several car journeys to Milan to visit my sister and her family. We explored France, Germany and Switzerland, taking different routes every time. As we camped most of the time, we had the freedom to find interesting and stunning places. There were no major motorways as we know them now – only main roads that went through little villages. Petrol stations were few and far between so one had to be very organized. Making 'phone calls often proved complicated as we never seemed to have the right change. (You guessed it, no credit cards). Card payments did exist, but not for telephone boxes.

We never knew what we would discover each day but the one thing we were always sure of was freshly baked bread at 6 am every morning in the campsites! We even found a chip machine in the campsite at Lake Titisee in Switzerland. How does a machine produce hot, fresh chips all by itself?

We occasionally came unstuck when we took the little 'white roads' marked on the map. One time, it was in Switzerland, near the St Julier Pass. The route looked interesting on the map and also a sort of short cut. We were in the Alps, albeit in summer, and surrounded by craggy mountains and spectacular scenery. On our left, the road clung to the mountainside, with a sheer drop into a bottomless valley to the right. It looked reasonably well made to start with, so we happily set off to explore. As we drove further along, the surface of the road began to deteriorate, with potholes and little piles of stones. Still, there was nowhere to turn the car around, so we carried on, thinking that this would surely have not been marked as a road if it did not go somewhere. We then noticed that the low barrier wall on the right had completely disappeared. A slight wave of panic came over us. There really was no choice but to very slowly and very carefully keep going.

Jehan's driving skills were tested to the full, as was the trusty red Audi which obeyed his every touch. I watched the stones disappear off the side of the road into the deep chasm. The road was only wide enough for one car. Just. Being the ultimate optimist, I cheerfully comforted him by saying that at least nobody would be coming along in the opposite direction! After what seemed like hours, during which we had aged ten years, the road improved and we found civilization. We also saw a big notice saying 'Road closed due to Landslide'. It might have helped to have the notice at the other end!

When Jehan's parents Amy and Kaiky came to visit us in England, we took them with us on a tour of Europe. They had spent their honeymoon in Europe in 1939 – the year war broke out. In fact, they were in Vienna when the news came. The honeymoon had to be cut short and they rushed back to the safety of India. We took them to the Vatican City in Rome. We also went to Assissi, Pisa, Florence and of course, Milan and Lake Como. It was a wonderful trip and the art and sculpture everywhere in Italy has to be seen to be believed. It is almost too much to take in all at once. We have made many more visits since and will continue to do so.

Amy dearly wanted to visit the Cathedral of Lourdes in the French Pyrenees, so we drove there from Rome to see what it was all about. This was quite an experience. Lourdes was the place where a young girl called Bernadette claimed to have seen the Virgin Mary standing by a spring of water. The vision told her that the water from this source would cure every known ill, and a cathedral must be constructed on the site so that people could come and be healed by the miraculous waters. This was done, and Bernadette became a saint. Thousands of Catholic and non-Catholic pilgrims and tourists flock to Lourdes throughout the year in the hope of eternal life and good health. Some do, indeed, go home much improved in health, if much poorer in wealth.

Chapter 8: Springing Off with Offspring

After six years of happy messing about, we finally decided to start a family. On the 1st of April 1976 our first son, Daraius, was born at St. James' hospital, Balham. Our lives changed completely and we were delighted with our extremely lively and handsome little boy. (Little being the operative word, as he weighed only 5 ½ lbs when he was born – one of a twin which sadly, we lost). We had begun a new adventure and, as nobody teaches you how to be a parent, it was a surprise-a-minute experience. Like changing a boy baby's nappy for the first time. They can pee in your face with great accuracy. He really was fun from the word 'go' and still is. (Doesn't do the nappy thing anymore). We took him everywhere with us, camping in the great outdoors and he took his first steps, aged 1, on the Isle of Wight. Our delightful second son, Jamsheed, arrived two and a half years later on the 3rd January 1979. It was snowing heavily when we got to St. George's hospital in Tooting just in time for 7.30 am. He weighed in at 7 ½ lbs and was another happy bundle of fun.

Children might be exhausting but they are exhilarating, too. Working from home, I was lucky enough to be with them all the time and enjoy their hilarious remarks. They grow up too quickly!

Jamsheed   Daraius

As Jehan worked shifts at the bank, there were times when he was on night duty, so keeping everything quiet during the day was quite a challenge. There was, however, the bonus of having him around on his days off. I carried on with my dress designing and we started the 'Craft Show circuit'. These were usually held over a weekend at wonderful locations, and, more often than not, a stately home in the country. We would travel up daily or stay at a B&B nearby, with the children in tow, unless my parents were around to babysit. The shows were held in huge marquees, so we would set up our stall alongside other craftspeople, some of whom were incredibly talented. Visitors and exhibitors would come from miles around regardless of the weather.

Selling glamorous silk dresses and jackets, in a marquee which smelled of wet grass, to ladies wearing wellies, is a strange image, but that's what we did. It was all hugely successful and we also made some good friends in the creative arts circle. Our home is now full of paintings and sculptures by various friends, including John Letts, a brilliant sculptor, and Sam Samaraweera, whose paintings were magnificent with the finest detail. We feel very lucky to have known them. John Letts started Jehan into sculpting, for which he discovered a real talent. John gave Jehan a little lump of terracotta clay, and Jehan, having never sculpted anything before, promptly modelled an exquisite bust of John himself. This led to bigger things. His first commission was to make a version of Rodin's Thinker for one of my friends, whose husband was a psychotherapist. This turned out to be so successful that Jehan had withdrawal symptoms when he had finished it and made another one for us to keep! We now have Rodin's Thinker-a-la-Jehan, which is a much better looking bloke than the original in Paris. Also some attractive nude ladies, for which he used his imagination...

There was one show at Wembley Stadium when I sold out my entire stock. I was making silk kaftans at the time (all the rage in the early 80s) and, having sold the one I was wearing, I subsequently sold every one of the next six I put on, along with other things (talk about selling the shirt off your back)! Craft Shows were a novelty at the time – now they are everywhere. I was still holding my dress parties at the time but becoming a bit ambitious, too. How nice it would be, I thought, to have my creations on sale in Oxford Street. So, without knowing the first thing about the wholesale rag trade, I made up a set of sample garments in colourful cotton sari fabric that I had brought back from a trip to India. There was a Kaftan, a short tunic top, a skirt and a matching frilly top. They were simple designs and very effective. I then rang the Fashion Buyer at Top Shop in Oxford Street and managed to get an appointment, saying that ours (mine) was a small company and just setting up in business, so would appreciate being able to show them my designs for their opinion. Jehan thought I was mad, but nevertheless, drove me into London for the appointment.

I showed the samples to two glamorous ladies wearing the highest heels I'd ever seen. They asked me if my company could handle a small order. I said, 'Oh Yes'. (thinking all the time of the spare bedroom and my one sewing machine and me). So they ordered 12 dozen of each of the four items on display. This was, of course in department store terms, a small order. With my rudimentary knowledge of maths, I worked out that this was 144 of each. I gulped discreetly, and asked how soon they expected these to be in the shop. 'Now' was the answer. It was February and I had thought that Summer stock would not be required till summer!! That's how much I knew. So, without a tremble or a wobble, I said 'Will three weeks do?' They said that would be fine, but one week would be better.

So I took the order and left the office, walking on a cloud at least six feet in the air.

How I was going to manage this, I had no idea. I did not even have enough fabric in stock. When I got back to the car, speechless and hugely excited, Jehan shrugged his shoulders and said – 'You'll do it!' And we did. I advertised in the local newsagent for a couple of local machinists, rang a business friend in India to rush the fabric over, and worked day and night to get the order done. I also had to order labels for the fabric content etc. and make a proper designer label. Unbelievably, all was ready and perfect and delivered in pristine condition within two weeks. They sold within the next two weeks and I was asked for some more.

The following year, I went to Dickins and Jones in Regent Street as by now, I was a bit more au fait with how things worked. I had found some fabulous plain white cotton sari fabric with pastel coloured borders. This was a completely different look from the one we had previously, and much prettier. This time I was prepared, and got quite a large order. A couple of days after we delivered them, the buyer rang me. I panicked, thinking something had gone wrong. It was just to say that they were going to display my designs in their Regent Street window alongside some very expensive French Swimwear, so if I'd like to come and take a few photographs, I would be very welcome. This was the ultimate joy. After that, I decided I had got it out of my system and went back to doing the dress parties and craft shows as they were much easier to handle!

Streatham was lovely when we first lived there, but then Brixton had major riots and it wasn't that far away. The neighbourhood was slipping. The final crunch came when, one afternoon, we had invited some highly respectable friends to lunch and a completely naked woman, high on drugs, came dancing down the road. Police officers arrived, not knowing where to put their helmets. The area was turning a bit rough, so we decided it was time to move. We saw several houses in and around Esher, in Surrey, and one of these was a flat above three shops in Esher High Street. It was a lovely old property with a charming garden. The idea of opening a shop in such a lovely area was most appealing, as it also took the rent from the other two shops. The flat seemed big enough at the time. We put a deposit down on it, but our buyer pulled out at the last minute, so the deal fell through and we were most disappointed. However, before they moved, the lovely owner held a dress party for me, to introduce us to her friends and the area in general.

There, I met Barbara, who made fabulous outfits in suede. She is a bubbly, enthusiastic and very creative lady and immediately suggested we join forces and so, 'Suede and Silk' was born. We became, and still are, very good friends. A month after the previous deal with the Esher house had fallen through, we had a firm buyer for our house, and one morning we had a 'phone call from Barbara. A friend of hers who was a divorcee with three girls was marrying a widower with three boys, and her house in Claygate was therefore, for sale. It was, apparently, in one of the prettiest roads in Claygate. Barbara insisted that we go and see the house immediately and even arranged the visit.

We went – and fell in love instantly with the house, the location and the giant willow tree on the green in the middle of Meadow Road. Barbara's friend had laid out tea on the lawn with, no less, cucumber sandwiches, and coming down from urbanised Streatham, this was pure seduction and a taste of country living. The garden was very pretty and the fact that all three bedrooms were decorated in violent shades of pink, blue and peach did not worry us at all!

with Barbara

It was June and all was beautiful. We made up our minds overnight and I think we rang and made the owner an offer at 7.30 am. The offer was accepted and what is more, the vendors gave us the keys and said we could decorate before we moved in with our furniture, as the house would be empty. The contracts had not yet been signed and no money had changed hands. Nowadays, people wouldn't dream of trusting anyone like that. The brilliant neighbours had a party to introduce us to everyone else in the road and we made new friends straightaway. We owe Barbara a great debt for pushing us in the right direction!

Daraius joined Esher Church School and Jamsheed joined the Catholic nursery school at the Arbrook Hall. We are neither Catholic nor C of E but religion has never made the slightest difference to us. When they were eight years old, they both went to Claremont Fan Court School in Esher, which was a Christian Science School. It seemed just the right place for them and they flourished. The fees there were pretty steep, but just as our parents had spent all they could afford on our education – we realised that this was the greatest gift a parent can give, along with time and of course, love. Perhaps they would have performed as well in a State School – perhaps not – but we've done it, now. Nobody teaches you to be a parent and it's different for everyone. Apart from the (often sound) advice your own parents give you, and which you invariably ignore and think you know better, you're on your own. It is quite normal not to value our parents' advice until they are long gone and then it's too late.

Dad on his 74th Birthday with Jamsheed & Daraius

During the children's school years, life carried on as busy as ever. I worked from home, designing, sewing and organising Fashion Shows for charity. The first ever Fashion Show was at Esher Church School to raise funds for school projects. Barbara and I made a collection of super outfits. This was the knickerbocker era and the lovely Princess Diana. Perish the thought. No woman, apart from the Princess, should have been allowed to wear knickerbockers. I remember making some bright emerald green ones in silk and the lady who modelled them, bought them. I think they had some gold trim on them too. This was the first of many shows.

Since 1982 there has been a show or two every year for some charity or another, with each show raising an average of £1000. Over the years, that is a lot of money raised for cancer research, various school equipment projects, the 1st Claygate Scout Group, Claygate Village Association and the Princess Alice Hospice among them. To date, we have put together something like fifty shows. There were lots of models and volunteers who willingly gave up their time and talents to help with the music and lighting. Jehan and I would organise it all, and I designed all the outfits. There would be around 80 ensembles for each show, which went on for 1½ hours with an interval. I would design, cut, sew and finish each one myself. I had lots of clients, so to make things easy, I would often ask them to model outfits that I had made for them, plus some new ones. It was ridiculously hard work but when you were as obsessed with fashion and sewing as I was, it was fun. It would not be unusual to find me putting the finishing touches on something at 4 am.

The very first Fashion Show in 1982

There is great personal satisfaction in hard work, which produces great results. The shows became part of the village calendar and were looked forward to every year, being a thoroughly community event. By now, all the models had become good friends, and more or less ran the show themselves! They performed to live musical accompaniment, which was provided by local talent, as we appeared to be surrounded by accomplished musicians in Claygate. The standard was pretty high, considering some of the highly professional fashion shows we have been to. We even had delicious homemade refreshments, made by Dot (Claygate's answer to Mary Berry), in the interval and plenty of wine. Perhaps it wasn't just the clothes that brought in the crowds!

Fashion Show 2012 - 30 years on and still going strong!

Chapter 9: Joining Scouting Unprepared!

When Daraius turned eight, we thought he should join the Cub Scouts with the 1st Claygate Scout Group. At the open evening, the Group Scout Leader mentioned that they were very short of leaders but had a long waiting list of boys, so needed some more volunteers. I promptly put my hand up and said I would help in any way required. Everyone stared in amazement. I could detect looks of pity and admiration but could not distinguish which was which. My offer of help was received with huge appreciation and before I knew it, I was receiving a warrant and being invested as a Cub Scout Leader.

I had never even been in the Guides and did not have a clue as to what was involved but was always ready and willing to learn. The only problem was, the other leaders expected me to know a lot more than I did, which resulted in many hilarious incidents. One of these concerned the construction of a wet pit at camp. To build a wet pit, you dig a hole in the ground, take three sturdy poles and make a tripod with some strong string, and suspend a black bin bag with tiny holes to drain the liquid from the food waste that you throw in the top. You then dispose of the drained rubbish in the bin and fill the hole back up before you leave camp, so there is no trace. Simple. Well, about six months after I had joined, we acquired a cheerful new leader and I thought I'd take him under my wing and show him the ropes as nobody had done that with me. So, at his first camp, we undertook to make the wet pit – a job nobody else rushed forward to do.

Having dug the hole, we set off to find some poles. Stashed in the corner of the main marquee, we found three matching poles of the right size and a neatly wound ball of string. The string was in bits with knots in it, so we found a knife to cut it all to the right size. Off we went and proudly constructed the finest wet pit you ever did see. Soon after, we saw John, our Group Scout Leader, looking very preoccupied and agitated. He kept saying, 'It's got to be here somewhere, I know we packed it'. We had no idea what he was looking for so took no notice. Suddenly, he saw the wet pit. We proudly went up and claimed responsibility for making it. He peered a bit closer, then he said – 'that's where it is! That's the blooming flag pole!' Now, constructing a flag pole at camp requires a great deal of skill, as the lengths of string to put it together and hoist and lower the flag have to be very accurate, as do the poles. This had all been beautifully and painstakingly prepared by John and completely destroyed by us. Apart from the great indignity of turning our revered flag pole into a wet pit.

We meekly took it all apart, suppressing our giggles, and the next morning when we assembled to salute the flag, a little teabag was found tied to the hoist.

Every Tuesday was Cub night, regardless of weather. I went to various training camps to learn new skills to teach the cubs and there were at least three major camps during the year, two in tents and the summer camp in a building at one of the many wonderful campsites we have in the South of England. 1st Claygate Scout Group began in 1906 and the mode of transport then was horse and wagon but we had progressed to a bright yellow minibus. Summer camp usually had thirty-six boys aged 8 – 11, so was a hugely energetic, action packed week.

There were Group Shows (Gang shows, as they were called – begun by Ralph Reader). These spectacular productions were organised by our Group Scout Leader, John Baldwin. A more devoted, enthusiastic and committed leader I have yet to meet. Every child and leader took part in these shows whether they wanted to or not. It was usually the most reluctant ones who shone and wanted to do it all over again. I helped organize four Group Shows, which were a very big affair with a cast of around two hundred. This involved the entire Scout Group, from Beavers aged 6 to Venture Scouts aged 18 and all the Leaders. Chaos. Lots of rehearsals, lots of panic, lots of costumes to be made on a shoestring, songs to be composed and sung, short plays and complicated dance routines.

The idea of the Group Show was to build confidence, teach discipline and team work and generally raise morale. There were no girls in the Scout Group at that time, so all the female parts would have to be played by the boys. They did not need much persuading, and the vision of 'The Ascot Gavotte' from 'My Fair Lady' will stay with me forever. We had six, elegant 8 year old cubs dressed in black and white long frocks and large hats and parasols, dancing with six grey suited little gentlemen in top hats. We drew the line at allowing them to stuff socks down the front of their dresses. I often wondered what profession these children would follow when they grew up. Many years later, much to my delight their parents still keep me informed, and we have police inspectors, politicians, doctors and television presenters among them. Our own two little cubs have made hugely successful and happy lives of their own, with Daraius becoming a brilliant Scout Leader himself, joining as I did, many years later, when his eldest was eight.

By the time we were in our forties, we had made so many trips to France and the rest of Europe, that we thought it might be fun to buy a little house in France as a base for our holidays. Somewhere rural and which needed a bit of work – the dream of doing up a French ruin. So began another grand adventure, and it all started with a meringue.

Except that we didn't have much money, of course, so it had to be very cheap and very cheerful. With this pie in the sky idea we decided to look into the possibilities seriously.

We spoke to people, read books on France and as all our holidays seemed to be camping in various parts of France, we learned a bit more as we went along. We also learned that even in the late eighties, any property that cost in the region of £7000 (then 70,000 French Francs) didn't have a roof, a floor or any running water, let alone an access road to it. Nevertheless, optimistic to the last, we contacted an English estate agent in the Cevennes and went to meet him and his wife in the remotest parts of the wild mountains of the south of France. We were totally honest with him regarding our meagre budget, and were quite prepared to be sent packing. To our delight, they were perfectly charming and said they were going to see some likely properties that day for evaluation, and it would be no trouble (indeed, a pleasure) to take us along and we could have a picnic somewhere along the river.

We told the kids we were going house-hunting and they said "Boring!" but oh, what fun it turned out to be. These lovely people took us to see three magnificent properties, described in true estate agent language. 'Private and secluded' meant that it was ten kilometres off the road which itself was little more than a dirt track. 'Character dwelling' probably referred to the house that had the old lady in it, complete with gout and a bad temper Was the old lady being sold off with the property? Now, there's an idea – I have a couple of cantankerous old aunts (no, maybe not). I could not help but feel sorry for Madame – stuck so far away from civilization (or so it seemed). All around us were deep woods and I could not see any telephone lines.

The Cevennes is a particularly rugged and densely forested area, rich in wildlife with steep mountain tracks, which make many parts of it inaccessible. Long may it remain so. We felt it would be foolhardy to consider such an extremely remote location. Suppose one had to get to a hospital in a hurry? Suppose the car broke down? No telephone, no mobile phones or signals, as they did not exist in those days. With two young children, and not having been brought up in the Australian outback, we didn't think this would be a good idea. Mind you, Jehan grew up in East Africa and has a vast knowledge of survival skills, having also become a Queen's Scout. Nothing seems to baffle him – he always finds a way around things. It's the 'Nothing is impossible or unworkable' theory. Thank goodness he's got me. Read into that what you will.

As we were visiting in August during school holidays, any sources of water were fairly dry and some of these houses had no mains connections. Electricity? Well, we could certainly manage without that – no French Television – Yippee! (You can't say that, I hear you say. Well, we are part of the EC now so that must count towards freedom of speech about European countries. Since we're all one big family we are only making fun of ourselves, and that's alright).

Oh well, back to the house business. One property had a special historic connection. There was a Huguenot grave in the garden (complete with occupant) and every year the villagers made a pilgrimage to it, so that was part of the deal. Now that's different. Fancy having your own personal cemetery as a garden feature – maybe those garden makeover programmes could pinch the idea. How trendy is that? However, we had a lovely day with these super people but none of these amazing places quite fitted the bill (literally), as they were all double what we could realistically afford. Add to that the huge amount of work and money that would be needed to restore them to a comfortable standard. We took our hosts out to dinner at a lovely restaurant in the middle of nowhere to thank them for all their efforts to enlighten us on the joys of holiday house hunting in France.

Here I must make mention of the gourmet French cuisine, more of which follows later, but in this instance 'gourmand' was the case, as the quantities of steak and chips had us all, including the boys, defeated and so we parted company with our hosts on a full and happy note.

By this time our lads, Daraius the older one, full of enthusiasm for the great outdoors and Jamsheed the younger and quieter one, were truly bitten by the house hunting bug – what with picnics and swimming in the rivers – trout tickling optional. We carried on looking in estate agents windows, albeit half-heartedly now, because we realised that finding anything at the price we were thinking about was almost impossible, but nevertheless, no harm in looking.

In the second week of our holiday we decided to explore the Pyrenees, as there were reputedly some cheaper properties around there. We discovered wonderfully secluded villages in the mountains and the scenery was absolutely stunning everywhere you looked. Pine forests, crystal clear mountain streams and clean crisp air. Fantastic walking country – this was high summer but the air was cool and fresh. The river water was icy cold – no skinny-dipping picnics here, then. There were some lovely old properties tucked away in beautiful forest locations but the whole idea was to have a holiday house in sunshine and heat, which was definitely in short supply here. However, if one was into skiing, there were plenty of easily accessible winter resorts.

We did go in search of a couple of houses, one of which was most memorable because we almost never got to it. It was situated in a little village, which we cleverly found by following our map – as you do - and drove into the main square. The car we had at the time was a huge white Citroen CX Safari estate. It was like an enormously comfortable, overstuffed sofa on wheels with a bonnet the size of a snooker table. The French used these cars as ambulances then and I think they still do.

The estate agent had sketched us a little map of the village, indicating the house we wished to see. On entering the square we needed to take the second left and then the first right and 'voila' there would be the house at the end of the street. What he had omitted to mention was that we should park in the village square and walk. Expertly, we turned into the second left as instructed, gazed at by a couple of old ladies clutching their baguettes. The road narrowed slightly and two more old ladies on chairs outside their houses tucked their feet out of the way as we rolled past. They carried on knitting as their eyes followed us down the road. Ah - first right coming up, quite a tight corner but phew, just made it. By now, some young children had arrived on the scene too, and a few more chaps in blue overalls. We smiled at everyone and slowly drove on. Our smiles were met with blank expressions – well, not quite blank, more bemused. The road was getting narrower by the second, but it was not until both the front tyres were scraping the kerbs of the very narrow pavements that we realised we were truly in the *merde*, with the entire population of the village discussing the situation.

Sure, we'd found the house alright but the road ended there and apart from being air lifted by a very big helicopter, the only way out was backwards. Added to this was the fact that we couldn't actually open the doors to get out, so there was nothing for it but to take a few long, deep breaths and smile.

The village came to life that day. The café emptied – games of *boules* were left unfinished, people in wheel chairs were brought out to see the entertainment. The Circus had come to town in the form of a large white Citroen Safari with a GB sticker and a foolish family of city slickers who didn't have the common sense to park in the village square and walk.

I mentioned earlier that Jehan always gets us out of difficulties. Seeing that he got us into this one in the first place, he calmly said 'What goes in must come out given that all measurements remain the same'. Perfectly logical, as the car and the street (though full of onlookers by now) were still the same size, so all he had to do was reverse in exactly the same tracks as he came in. This would require bending the laws of physics for driving, as the steering wheels were now on the back of the car. An impossibility! To helpful shouts of *'Allez!'* and *'Arretez!'* and occasionally *'Hop-la!'* and *'Boum!'* he slowly and dexterously extricated the car from its predicament – with nothing damaged except perhaps a bit of dignity.

There was hearty applause all round with lots of smiling faces, but you could hear them thinking *'Les stupide Anglais'* and if our boys had considered disowning us before, all was now forgiven. Their dad was a great driver. Needless to say we didn't pursue a house in that particular village – too embarrassing!

Chapter 10: Finding Joumeyrac

Having decided against the cold of the Pyrenees we dejectedly headed north for Dover as the return ferry was booked for the Saturday evening. On Friday Jehan said he would like to visit the town of Millau and the Gorges du Tarn in the Aveyron, as it was a very beautiful region of France. So we made a little detour and that was it. Absolutely stunning scenery almost too beautiful to describe – hillside villages clinging to the rocks – water falls, lush greenery, warmth – just about everything good about France. Wanting to spend more time here, we decided to make this spot our next holiday destination. This is where the meringue came in.

We stopped in the town of Millau to exchange some travellers cheques and while Jehan was in the bank I took the boys along to get something to eat and bought some huge meringues. Waiting for Jehan to come back I spotted an estate agent's window and through force of habit ran my eye over the pictures and prices. In one corner there was a sun-faded photograph of a red roofed cottage sitting by itself in the middle of some spectacular countryside. It said –'Une petite maison avec 2.5 Hectares du terrain – 75,000FF'. Which by easy calculation was roughly £7500, which was ridiculously cheap compared to what we had seen, so there had to be a catch. Maybe the photo had been in the window for the past twenty years – it certainly looked it!

So, tempted to simply ignore it as a mirage, I showed it to Jehan and the sort of chap he is, he said "Well, let's go and ask" – so, feeling very silly and thinking 'well no one knows us here anyway' we gingerly went up two flights of stairs to this seedy looking office and asked the dozy gentleman with the moustache about this house for 75,000 FF. He didn't even bother putting out his Gauloise which seemed to be growing out of the corner of his mouth but simply shrugged his shoulders and shoved a photocopy of the route to the house towards us and said "Well, there's no electricity and no mains water and it's almost a ruin, but you can go and have a look if you can find it." Which didn't sound very promising but the sort of idiots we are – we said "Okay!" and off we went. He presumably then went home to complete his nap, not imagining that we'd ever come back.

We jumped into the car, map in hand and found the road along the river going out of Millau. It was a sultry summer afternoon. The level of the river was very low and it looked cool and inviting in the blazing heat. The road was tarmacked but very rough – obviously not used a lot. We drove along in anticipation looking for the magic house in the sun-faded photograph, passing through several sleepy villages, disturbing the dogs and admiring the magnificent scenery. There were thickly wooded mountains all around us and high up we could see caves, seemingly inaccessible. At long last, after passing through the village of Candas with all the houses shuttered down for the afternoon, we saw a tiny signpost for Roquetaillade. In spite of the name it clearly did not merit a larger signboard.

The road narrowed even further before starting to climb steeply. There was another river on our left – the Muse – which joined the Tarn at the little bridge we had just passed, The view was still spectacular as the valley opened up below us. There were several stone ruins scattered about and terraces built into the mountainside. This was once a fairly important wine producing area, but after the great decimation of French vineyards by Phylloxera in the last century, it never revived. Being the height of summer, it was hot and still and very dry. We saw a buzzard sitting in a tree, even he was too hot to fly around. On we went round several bends, hugging the mountainside on the right, in case some inebriated French driver came hurtling round the corner – after all it was after lunch time. Worse still, a French cyclist. Forget mad dogs and Englishmen, here it's buzzards and *bicyclistes* in the noonday sun, complete with tight shorts and racing bike.

At one point we saw a house deep in the valley approximately five hundred yards vertically down from the road with absolutely no access. It was in deep shade from the mountain wall behind and it was '*à vendre*'. An aerial pulley system, now rusting away, was visible from the road. No, this wasn't the one we were looking for. It didn't have a red roof and it looked truly dismal. It also looked as if it had been for sale for at least fifty years as even the sign was rotting away. Not surprising, what fool would build a house down there? Of course, we realised later that the original track to Roquetaillade from St. Hippolyte at the bridge would have been along the river, therefore these houses would have been built at intervals along the track, now only negotiable on foot. So we carried on up the hill to Roquetaillade.

Another sign post, a big one this time, to the left, down into another valley. We crossed a tiny bridge over the river Muse and found ourselves in what must be the village square. Apart from the church there was nothing. No café, no post box, no telephone box, no bar, no nothing, except a bottle bank in the shape of a large old oil drum and the communal wheelie bin. The main part of the village was to the right but our directions were to turn left up the other side of the valley, so we did.

Well, we found the house. Or, at least, we could see it – tantalisingly charming, like Little Red Riding Hood's grandma's cottage, sitting all by itself in a valley about a hundred yards from the road as the crow flies. But not being crows and not even having wings for that matter, we couldn't find a way down to it at all. Like grandma's cottage and Sleeping Beauty's castle rolled into one, it was surrounded by thick brambles and evil looking weeds as high as your eye, all the way up to the road. So, continuing further up the road round to the back we found ourselves behind and above the house, which was now out of sight in the valley below. With great determination, wearing shorts and Tshirts we painfully negotiated a path down. On reaching the house, we realised that there was a little stream bed running down in front of it, which one crossed by a tiny bridge and that there was a fairly steep but accessible pathway to it from the front. And oh, it looked so appealing. No doors, no windows – it was in the first stage of renovation – it had the roof. A red roof with lovely old fashioned *Tuiles de Marseilles.*

With walls of stone three feet thick, the house was built over a cave. Imagine an overhang of rock under which stone-age man made a dwelling – a proper cave. Then the walls of the cave had been extended with large painstakingly chosen stones and the roof of the cave extended into an arched vault with a beautiful doorway, the stones having been cut to shape. The main part of the house was on top of the cave, the back wall being sheer rock like the cave. The flooring above was newly laid concrete, with no way down to the cave from inside the house.

Inside, we found a pile of sand, an old wooden ladder and a bird's nest. It was so quiet and so isolated and yet, the village of

Roquetaillade was less than half a kilometre away on the other side of the mountain – well within walking distance. The five acres of land that came with the house, was in the form of three stepped fields behind the house, two fields in front and a lot of woodland up and down the stream. Except that the stream was completely dry. There was not a puddle of water to be seen, not even a damp patch. This did not look good. Without water nothing is possible.

Having got completely excited about the project which was like a dream come true – small enough to handle and work on by ourselves with enough land to mess about on, we had to look carefully into the water situation. Both boys were very enthusiastic about the idea but, never having been on Disneyworld/Centre Parks type holidays, they didn't know any better and thought that this was what normal families did for their holidays. Which was just as well because they were a great help in working on the house as they grew up.

We rushed back to the estate agent only to find that he was, *naturellement,* shut. So all we could do was continue on our way back to England. We rang him en route the next morning to ask him if there was water on the land. Was the stream usually flowing? He replied 'Yes' and we asked for all the details to be sent on to us in England, which he duly did. Even so, Jehan and I came back in November 1989 with a friend who spoke fluent French to take another look at the water supply. We couldn't cross the little stream! The water was flowing half a metre over the bridge and further downstream there was our very own waterfall in a deep ravine, complete with ferns and probably fairies.

The vendor, Michel, with the estate agent in tow, came to meet us at the house and we stood on the road surveying the land. Spreading out the map on the bonnet of the car, we asked him, "Where exactly is the boundary of the land?" he said, "Start from this tree here and go in a straight line to the top of the mountain" so we said, "And if this tree should fall down, where would the boundary be then?" to which he replied, "Oh well, to the next tree, I guess." So, on his assurance that there was always a source of water on the land, we took a deep breath, shook hands and sealed the deal with this delightful man with the twinkling eyes.

In France, the system is that you pay 10% of the asking price when you decide to buy, which is forfeited if you back out. The remainder of the payment is made within three months in a *notaire's* office with both parties present. It is a very fair and organised system with no complicated delays. When we returned in February 1990 to complete the transaction, Michel and Ginette (the vendors) insisted we stayed with them and looked after us like old friends. I can hear some suspicious minds thinking 'So what *was* wrong with the house?' Well – nothing. They were just nice people and I guess they thought we were pretty nice too and a little bit crazy.

By the time we arrived, Michel had already laid pipes to the house from a source of water three hundred metres upstream. He had also dug a large hole and installed a *fosse septique* (septic tank). All the basics were in place, and all we needed were windows, doors, a toilet, a washbasin, taps, tables, chairs, beds, a kitchen sink and a few other essentials to make a home.

During the May half term holidays we decided to tackle the most important job, which was to install the bathroom. As we did not know where to find all the paraphernalia in a new place and had only a short time to get things done, the decision was to take most things down with us in our trusty white Citroen Safari estate, loading it up with a loo, a cistern, a wash basin, all the piping and connections necessary, camping equipment, four Z-beds, four chairs and a table, kitchen utensils and, on the roof rack, amongst other things, a kitchen sink! Yes really. One would think we were venturing into the wilds of Africa, not modern state-of-the art France. We left, much to the amusement of our neighbours in leafy Claygate, looking like the Beverly Hillbillies.

By now, Michel had installed a beautiful front door, another solid wood arched door to the *Cave* and also the windows. We had left all the choosing to him and he chose well. He considered this house as his baby and kept an eye on it when we were not there, checking up on any jobs we did, approving or disapproving freely. We set to work constructing the bathroom, and bearing in mind the connections to the new *fosse*, the only logical place was in the *cave* where the walls are mountain rock, *au naturel*, with ledges to put your soap and shampoo on – it's really quite different. When it rains heavily water runs down the rock face on the back wall and forms a little stream, which flows out from under the door, just as it must have done for many decades.

Our first priority was a flushing toilet and never having tackled a job like this before, it was a source of great entertainment. The first job was to build a breezeblock platform to site the loo on. This we did quickly and smartly without ever thinking of a spirit level. Result? A slightly sloping loo. You learn not to take things for granted here. We did not realise the adverse camber of the loo until the next day by which time the cement was well and truly set and the tiling in place. So there we have it – everything else in the house is almost as nature intended so why not our new white flushing toilet. The cistern then had to be attached to the wall. Simple enough, but when your walls are solid stone and you do not have an electric masonry drill, you think of alternatives. We discovered easy-fix Supermousse. No, it's not an instant dessert off the supermarket shelf that comes in little teaspoon size pots. It's a builder's superglue that comes in a high pressure gun. What we didn't know at the time was its power of expansion. We squirted it on and positioned the flush tank. It held beautifully.

Then the Supermousse started to come to life. It was everywhere, swelling and billowing out from behind the cistern like a living thing, sticking to the wall and making a huge mess. Had this happened at our house in England we would have been beside ourselves in horror. But here, in this *cave* in deepest Aveyron it was the weirdest sight. We watched in amazement until it finally stopped and then spent the best part of the day scraping it clean. I write this several years later and the tank is still in place without a single bracket holding it.

Chapter 11: French Frolics

Life has been an exciting journey, with something new and interesting happening all the time. We never seemed to stop. Our trips to France were always busy, too. We loved going down to Joumeyrac, as the house in Roquetaillade was called. There was always work to be done, but this would be alternated with swimming in the rivers, canoeing down the Tarn and barbecues with friends.

Something that had to be done quite urgently was to put shutters on all the windows. Now that this was to be a proper house, one had to make it secure when we were not here and wooden shutters were *de rigeur*. Jehan set about making these, as we could not buy the exact sizes readymade – the two big windows being of awkward sizes and also quite crooked. So he made them to measure, and fitted them with large strong hinges and bolts to the stone walls outside the glass windows. Which sounds pretty straightforward till you realise that there was no electricity, and at that time, no generator or cordless drill (which could not be charged up anyway) so it was hand drilling, hand sawing, hand everything.

The most difficult part was drilling into the stone by hand. We look back on it now and wonder how he managed it. They are beautiful shutters in weathered pine with all the traditional ironwork to go with them. It's surprising what new-found enthusiasm and youth can accomplish.

That first summer we cooked on a small Calor gas ring and slept on folding beds in sleeping bags. Apart from having a tiled roof over our heads we might as well have been on a campsite. The stream provided water for washing and bathing (and flushing the exotic toilet). Although a pipe had been laid from a water source further up the valley down to the house, we had no taps or sink in place. These were painstakingly installed bit by bit.

There was enough headroom inside the house to construct another floor, thus giving us a separate bedroom. We asked Michel for ideas and advice, gingerly suggesting he might consider doing this in our absence. When we returned later in summer, lo and behold – he had fixed thick wooden beams all the way from wall to wall and laid substantial floorboards, making a mezzanine floor. All that remained for us was to build a staircase to replace his makeshift wooden ladder.

Off we went to the timber yard with our design, had the treads and risers cut to exact sizes and, with all hands to the task, the staircase was glued and screwed and ready for a coat of varnish by the evening. We now had ourselves a second room and could seriously think about getting proper beds and mattresses. What a luxury that would be! The house was truly becoming a home.

On our very first morning in the new bedroom at Joumeyrac, we were woken by a herd of sheep bleating in the upper field behind the house. They were followed by a drunken shepherdess in a grubby pink cardigan and a tattered straw hat. She waved cheerfully and gave us a huge toothless grin. We waved back sleepily, thinking this was all a strange dream. Each morning this apparition arrived at precisely 5.30 am. We mentioned it to Michel who told us that our fields had been her grazing grounds for years. We said we didn't mind and would he please tell her she may continue to do so as we were not going to be here all the time. (I think she intended to continue anyway). However, the next time we came down from England, no shepherdess. It appears the drink got the better of her one evening and she stumbled, hit her head and died. So, sadly, we never really got to know her but we did get to lie in.

The following evening at about 5 pm, while pottering about outside the house, we saw, much to our amazement, striding through the undergrowth, a couple in pristine tennis whites complete with racquets and sweat bands. They walked up to the house and looked surprised to see us. We all stared at each other in astonishment. Then they said *'Bonjour!'* and we said *'Bonjour!'* and they carried on up the drive and onto the road. Then they vanished and we never saw them again. If the whole family had not been there to witness the visitation, nobody would have believed it. Considering there wasn't a tennis court within 20 miles, the mystery has never been solved. Anyone for tennis?

That first summer, we became acquainted with our resident wild menagerie, starting with the *Loirs*. These are Edible Dormice in English. Not that we would ever dream of eating them, although the Romans did, and Mrs. Beeton, apparently, has a recipe in her famous cook book. These are sweet and furry little creatures, like baby squirrels with big bushy tails, which hibernate nine months of the year. For the short time they are awake in summer, they emerge mainly at night.

Outside the *cave* there is a large walnut tree. Walnuts are what *loirs* like best. They are extremely curious animals and will come and peer at you while you are in the shower. One night, a baby *loir* fell into the toilet bowl and Daraius bravely fished him out while wearing a thick motorcycle glove, as *loirs* have very sharp teeth, which they use to crack open the walnut shells. Having got him out he sat the baby *loir* on a ledge, all wet and scruffy and we can only assume his mum came and fetched him as he wasn't there the next morning. However, he was there the next evening. Where? On top of the cistern. Again. So the rule is, put the lid down;

and believe me, if you have a predominantly male family, having pet *loirs* will work.

The *loirs* had hitherto confined their activities to the *cave*, which was quite acceptable. They added a touch of excitement to shower time. One night, however, we were woken by squeaky, scratchy sounds in the kitchen, in the main part of the house. Heaving a sigh we said, 'ruddy mice'; turned over and went to sleep. Early the next morning, on the way down to make some coffee while the house was still in semi-darkness, there was a rustling sound on top of the kitchen cupboard. We shone a torch and there, right in the middle, were two large eyes staring down at us in surprise. It was the cutest *loir* you ever saw. This was not good news. We realised it had come in down the chimney as there were gaps on either side of the flue. The problem was, being creatures of habit, there was no chance it would leave by the window which was conveniently next to the kitchen cupboard – it had to go out the way it came in. We decided to wait until the rest of the family were up before tackling the situation. Surely a bunch of supposedly intelligent humans could dispatch one little *loir* without too much trouble.

Everyone took up positions in an effort to usher it towards the chimney. It darted behind a mirror, tantalisingly crossing over the open window. The mirror moved this way and that taking on a life of its own. We did not want to hurt it in any way – why *loirs* get preferential treatment over mice, I don't know. It shot upstairs towards the chimney, sat on a ledge for a long time and then came back down – behind the mirror, over the lintel above the window and back to the kitchen cupboard. This performance went on for an hour and a half. We finally gave up, having done ourselves more injury than necessary in our effort to keep the *loir* in good health, and went out. On returning, it appeared to have left, so the top of the cupboard was cleaned, the shredded paper table cloth which had been used for nesting cleared up and the gaps around the chimney securely cemented up.

We did have the occasional mouse or two. One can't help that in the countryside as they were here first. And you've got to like spiders – all sizes. My sister and brother-in-law once came to stay overnight with us in Joumeyrac on their way to Spain from Italy. As soon as the car stopped, my sister leapt out saying ' Thank goodness we've arrived, he wouldn't stop the car, there's a spider in the car and he wouldn't stop!' I asked her how big the spider was and she indicated the size of a pinhead. So I said 'You don't like spiders then' and she shivered in disgust. Oh dear - I knew there was a large black spider that lived in the corner above their bed, but he never bothered anyone so we ignored him. I said no more and our spider must have known he'd be dead meat if he showed himself, so he didn't. I hope he didn't crawl into any of their luggage, as I haven't seen him since.

Whenever we related our tales of the French house to our friends, they shook their heads in pity and sorrow. Why on earth would anyone want to spend their holidays doing that? Because it really was fun. Also, living there was so intensely hands–on, you had to be aware of what you were doing all the time, as one thoughtless move could result in serious injury. There was no electricity and therefore no television. This meant that you had no chance to worry about the catastrophes happening all over the world. There was time to watch the dragonflies hovering above the stream, and at night, gaze at the millions of stars in a sky totally unpolluted with artificial light. We read, played board games and went on adventurous walks. That is, when we weren't mixing concrete or messing about with rocks.

I am sure that this complete change of lifestyle two or three times a year did us a lot of good. Returning home, we threw ourselves into village life with renewed energy and fresh ideas. The reason we could wangle these breaks in France was thanks to Jehan's shift work at the bank. When the boys were still at school we could only go in the holidays but as the years went by we found ourselves nipping off up to four times a year.

For a change of scene one January, very soon after we had bought Joumeyrac, we decided to go on a skiing holiday to Andorra. This was the choice of destination as it was incredibly cheap, compared to the posher ski resorts, and we thought it might be more sensible as an introduction. We thought it might be fun to go with our dear friends Maggie and Gordon and their two sons Alistair and Dominic. So, with great enthusiasm the flights were booked, ski suits and accessories were bought or borrowed and off we went to practise on the artificial ski slopes at Sandown Park in Esher. That should have taught me a lesson, but it was too late. All was prepared. All the others, especially the children, were naturals at skiing and Jehan, Maggie and Gordon seemed to cope admirably. I discovered something I was really bad at. I had bruises that resembled the maps of Africa and Australia all over. Oh well, the bruises would heal and practice would make perfect and I was going to conquer my fears and become a champion skier – ever the optimist.

We flew to Toulouse in France and then took a coach transfer to Andorra. It was very late when we arrived, with four sleepy, hungry and very crochety children in tow. The coach dropped us off at the bottom of a very long, steep slope and the driver pointed out the hotel at the top of the hill. We waited expectantly for a minibus, soon realised that none was coming and then picked up all of our luggage and trudged up the hill. It was one o'clock in the morning. The reception was in total chaos, as many other guests had also arrived late. We finally got the keys to our rooms on the third floor and as the one and only lift was not in operation, struggled up the stairs.

The beds were not made up but the linen was set out on them. That's when I discovered continental pillowcases, which are open at both ends. Gordon tried to close the open window in their room and the entire window came off in his hands. So he walked back downstairs with this window and stood in the queue behind a lady who had come down to complain that there was no toothbrush holder in her bathroom! Memorable moments. We had to be up and ready at 8 am to hire our skis and boots and start lessons. We were then split into groups according to ability. I was the only grown-up relegated to the baby class. Still, someone had to keep an eye on the kids!

It all turned out to be very good fun. There were plenty of good places to eat, but none better than the little café below the hotel. It was run by a delightful French couple who were, clearly, very proud of their home cooking. Every evening there was a delicious hot casserole and a rib-sticking dessert. As we ended the day absolutely ravenous, this went down very well. One night we reached our limit as they kept piling on the food, and when the huge chocolate cake arrived, especially made for us, we had to discreetly stuff pieces into our pockets because we did not want to offend them. It was the first and last time I will ever put chocolate cake into my pocket!

The ski trip was such fun that we went again, two families together, to Val Thorens in France. By this time, we sort of knew how to ski and the weather was stunning. It was slightly more upmarket than Andorra and sunning ourselves on the balcony following a Jacuzzi bath surrounded by snow was quite an unusual experience. I also caused a bit of excitement when I tumbled head over heels into the snow while flying down a slope. This acceleration was due to the fact that our instructor thought I was going too slowly, so I thought, 'I'll show him!' We are all grateful that there was not a rock where my head disappeared under the snow. When I opened my eyes, all I could see was blue ice. Happily, I was able to stand up and shake myself down having lost nothing except my dignity! (Oh, and my skis).

Chapter 12: Making new Friends and Meeting a Count

Our boys have always made us proud by whatever they did, barring a few unmentionable moments, which only meant they were normal teenagers. The school years went by in a flash and then they were at College. Daraius went to Esher College and Jamsheed to Woking. Daraius always had a business head on his shoulders. I well remember taking him to Garson Farm in Esher to pick our own peas. He was only six years old, but had discovered that you paid for your pickings by weight. So, when I turned round to see why he was being so slow, I saw him shelling the peas before they went in the plastic bag. I said 'Hey, you're not supposed to do that!' and he calmly replied 'Well, we're not going to eat the shells so why pay for the extra weight?' From then on I had no fears that he would ever starve. As a matter of interest, his first proper job was with Garson Farm when he was 16. He is now the Director of his own business and well respected in his trade. He also has a super family.

Jamsheed always knew he wanted to be a musician. When he sat at the piano at the age of five and picked out the theme from Dvorak's New World Symphony, we realised he'd also got the gift for playing the piano. Music has been his life, along with various acting roles in musical theatre. Both boys were in the 1st Claygate Scout and Guide Band almost from the day it first started up. At one stage, Daraius became Band Leader. He played the drums and Jamsheed played the euphonium, which went with his build. We have enjoyed innumerable performances, including Daraius playing Tweedledum (Alice in Wonderland), to Jamsheed playing Pharoah/Elvis (Joseph and his Technicolour Dreamcoat), to name a couple, from both boys, and have stacks of video tapes which now have to go onto DVDs or even USBs – technical progress has gone berserk. Having graduated with a Music and Media degree from Sussex University, Jamsheed went on to follow a career in music – composing music for computer games, films and performing at various venues. He is currently a piano entertainer for Holland America Line. This must be the finest way to see the world and do what you love in the process. It also gives his parents an excuse to go on cruises.

Our annual holidays to France were much looked forward to every year. The first summer, we caused a great deal of curiosity, as this house had been a ruin for such a long time and then on the market for a while. This was probably because nobody had been able to find it. There were only two or three cars going up the road, (and occasionally down), but they always stopped to stare at the house which, if nothing else, now had red geraniums on the windowsills. One brown VW camper van in particular always went very slowly up and down. Noticing it had a GB sticker on it, the boys were told that the next time they saw it cruising past, they were to wave madly to stop them and invite them down for a drink. Which they duly did. This was our first introduction to the cosmopolitan and multilingual community of the Aveyron. (For these purposes, Australian has been designated a separate language).

Margaret and Michael live in Australia, travel all over the world, and every year, for a rest, fly to London, pick up their camper van and come to Montjaux, where they live in a tiny *cabane* four kilometres up the road from us, also without electricity or running water. This was so when we first met them but now they also have a big house in Bournac with all the mod cons and the *cabane* is a weekend abode. They have lots of amazing stories to tell about their travels and adventures. They promptly invited us with true Aussie hospitality for a barbie at the *cabane* to meet some more interesting people, including Bob from Australia, his lovely Dutch wife Weis, John and Maureen and Dorothy and David from England. What brings so many different types together has always been a mystery. Life is strange, we can plan all we want, but certain events seem to be predestined.

One evening, our new friends took us to Marie-Therese's restaurant in Montjaux. This was an extraordinary affair. The restaurant was in her home with six tables and a set menu. The food was absolutely delicious, lovingly prepared with the finest ingredients. She was a lady who loved to cook and had turned her hobby into a small business, helped by her friend Therese. We found ourselves using the restaurant quite frequently after that first visit, and one evening were invited to dinner with the family, after which we all went to Therese and Max's house for coffee. Our new found French friends, naturally, did not speak any English at all so we worked hard on our French, often having to resort to making an intelligent face when being told some complicated story, sometimes saying 'Oui' when we should have said 'Non' and smiling with delight when we should have been serious. That's when they told the story again to make sure we had understood. I was amazed at their tolerance and patience. Perhaps it was because we were making the effort to speak French properly, or maybe they just felt sorry for us. Therese and Max have three lively daughters who took our boys under their wing, so they had a chance to sort out their French too, one way or the other. They have become very close friends since then and have even made a trip to England to visit us.

The summer Daraius finished his GCSE exams, we took him and his school friend Kevin to France with us, as Jamsheed had gone to Italy to visit my sister Feroza at Lake Como.

Kevin was a very pleasant lad who did not eat vegetables. Seriously, no tomatoes, no peas, no beans, potato chips maybe, no fruit either. His mother had warned us about this. As Kevin was sixteen at the time we could not do much except give him what he liked, which was white sauce with rice or pasta and meat. Try as we might to tempt him with juicy pineapple, crunchy apples and creamy avocado, nothing worked. So we decided to take him to Marie T's restaurant where she made the most beautiful selection of starters. Melon with Parma ham, tomato and mozzarella with basil leaves, pineapple rings with fresh cherries and hard-boiled egg and mayonnaise. Kevin ate the eggs. There was a lovely fillet steak to follow with fresh beans and a huge salad. Kevin had just the steak. How a child could reach the age of sixteen, be absolutely charming and outwardly healthy apart from his very spotty complexion, without ever eating a fruit or vegetable, I'll never know. We were defeated.

After the meal the boys asked if they could walk back home – six kilometres downhill in pitch darkness. It seemed safe enough, a few perilous drops along the way, but they would eventually roll down to the house. It just so happened that a neighbouring village further up the mountain was celebrating this summer night with a laser light show. All we could see were strange flashes in the sky moving from place to place as the lights played on the underside of the clouds. We thought nothing of it and drove back home to wait for the boys. Within ten minutes we heard this great clatter of footsteps running down the road. They had convinced each other in the lonely darkness that this was an alien invasion. Of course they knew it wasn't really, but just in case. Once your legs start running downhill in panic, it's hard to stop.

The view from Montjaux during the day is spectacular, but at night it is truly special. In the darkness, the village of Roquefort can be seen in the distance, illuminated by floodlights and looking like a Spanish galleon in full sail, a ghost ship in a dark sea, all lit up with nowhere to go. Roquefort nestles under a huge rock face, inside which are the famous caves which have just the right atmosphere to ripen their world renowned cheese. When I was a little girl (in India) I would hear grown-ups talking about Roquefort cheese with reverence – how delicious it was and above all, how expensive. It must have been near impossible to get in India anyway. You can imagine my excitement when I realised our holiday home was so close to Roquefort – the name conjured up all sorts of romantic images... So if you are ever in the area, drive up to Montjaux on a dark, moonless night and look out at Roquefort. It's the stuff adventure stories are made of.

From the beginning, our friends have shown us so much kindness. We were often given fresh vegetables from their *potagers* and one cold January, Max and Therese insisted we spent the first couple of nights with them till our house warmed up with the fire going. Then, during an unexpectedly cold October, Pierre turned up with two enormous sacks of coal for us – he thought we could use it immediately – and we did. Pierre is a charming gentleman who lives in Montjaux.

Every village has its characters, just as every family has its share of strange people. Montjaux had George and George had his cows. The white one, Margarita, he said, was for milk and the brown one, Martine, for coffee. He was quite witty, was George, but as he lived in close proximity to his cows, one was always reluctant to shake hands with him and, if you were female, even more reluctant to offer your cheek for a kiss. George's other claim to fame was that he owned several tractors, only one of which was actually working. One day there will be a Museum of Ancient Tractors in Montjaux. However, whenever help was needed or a community service to be done, George was your man. The general factotum, with an unhygienic finger in every pie, he was a very useful chap to know.

One summer evening, Max and Therese invited us to dinner to introduce us to a Count, whose family owns the beautiful Chateau de

Vezin, some thirty kilometres north of Montjaux. In the summer months he lives in the Chateau, which is open to visitors and constantly needs some work done on it. Large houses, romantic chateaux and grand palaces give more pleasure to those who visit and admire them than to those who own them, maintain them and pay the heating and electricity bills. We went along to see the Chateau, which was a splendid affair. It must be wonderful to be able to trace your ancestral history far back into the middle-ages and know that your family lived in the same chateau for that length of time. This Chateau has not changed hands since it was built. During the French Revolution the owners were not harmed, as they were kind and caring landowners to their tenants and workers.

The personal tour we were given was most enjoyable. The kitchen had all the original equipment from ages past with a huge refectory table which was lower than usual as its legs had to be amputated six inches from the floor due to the onset of wood rot. They occasionally hold medieval banquets here, roasting whole lambs in the enormous fireplace and baking bread in the ancient *four* (a stone bread oven). Nothing had been changed or modernised. They must have needed an army of domestics to cope with the daily living, with whole forests being cut down for firewood. What an incredibly hard life it must have been for the servants. The kitchen boy must have spent all his time stoking the fires, morning till night, every day of his life. Nothing has changed much – the stockbroker who goes into

London on the 8.15 and returns home on the 9.15 in the evening, every day of his life? Only a slight change in life style, but what else is different? One has to make a living one way or another.

During July and August there are concerts galore in all the villages around, mostly open air and free to all comers. These take place in the evenings at weekends and also weekdays, often beginning at 9 pm and continuing until 1 am. How do they get to work the next morning, I wonder? Maybe they don't. A concert advertised to begin at 9 pm does not necessarily mean they actually begin to play at that time – often the stage is still being set up and the band is in the restaurant having their dinner. They will start when they are good and ready. So, one hangs around hopefully and at about 10 pm, if one is lucky, things begin to happen. One time, when we were still waiting at 11.30, we gave up and went home.

On the occasions when they are well organised these concerts are very good, with talented musicians from all over the world. There is plenty to eat and drink and dancing in the streets, notwithstanding the odd 50cc teenage two wheeled pride-mobile, which splutters and whines through the crowd. These are family outings from the oldest to the youngest bopping away into the night. There are couples with babies and teenagers – all ages dancing together and having a good time. Bedtime rules clearly do not apply. In all the years that we have enjoyed these chaotic concerts there has never been any sign of bad behaviour or trouble. It could be that it wasn't noticed because we were beyond the behaviour threshold ourselves, but I don't think so.

One evening, in Viala du Tarn, there was a performance by a Russian folk music group in national costume with an array of unusual Russian musical instruments. We sat in rows on wooden benches in the village square and were transported to *La Russie* on a magic carpet of colourful music and dance. On another occasion it was the choir from Kings College Cambridge singing at Chateau Caze in the Gorges du Tarn. (They did start on time - but then, they were British). The relaxed French attitude to summer entertainment was clearly illustrated when we went a long way to the Abbaye de Sylvanes to hear a leading choir from Toulouse. The first half of the concert, for which the tickets were quite expensive, was the 'Messa di Gloria' by Puccini and the second half, after the interval, was to be a recital by a leading soprano. The orchestra was superb as were the vocalists and the acoustics in the lovely old abbey were exceptional so we looked forward eagerly to the second half of the concert. However, during the interval, a short announcement was made that the star performer would not be arriving after all, as she had a cold, so the concert was at an end. With a shrug of shoulders and a resigned universal sigh, the audience rose and made their way home. How did their forefathers ever organise a revolution?

Admittedly, half a concert was better than none at all.

A few kilometres below Viala du Tarn is the little village of Le Minier, so named because there used to be silver mines here in Roman times. The mine entrances are still visible and presumably there is still silver in 'them thar hills,' (phrase from Brer Rabbit, for those of you too young to know), as this was quite an important village in those days. Bushman Bob the man from Oz lives in a rambling old *manoir* at the end of the village, with a lovely red climbing rose and huge white Hydrangea bushes at the entrance. It's the sort of house you could get lost in, with various steps and rooms in strange places and the garden on top of what appears to be someone else's abode.

The place is in a constant state of renovation and would surely lose all its charm if it were to be completed. You enter into a small courtyard with an old millstone set in the paving. To your left is a huge barn with all manner of everything unusable piled high -- it's mostly something Bob offered to store for someone else, who then lost interest in it. To your right, stone steps lead up to a small veranda surrounded by the magnificent red climbing rose and several creepers. Two well worn and much loved loom chairs and a rickety wooden bench upon which there is always a basket of walnuts or a box of plums or something interesting Bob has been gathering. On the wall there is a little slate with a piece of chalk for visitors to write their messages – the original answer phone.

A door leads into the kitchen, with an impressive wooden dining table large enough to seat twelve, bunches of intriguing herbs hang drying from the ceiling. Several pairs of boots and shoes stand in a corner, in readiness for the steady stream of houseguests who may suddenly want to go on a long hike or perhaps skiing. The large cooking range always has something mysterious bubbling away in a big saucepan, and there is the tiniest ancient stone sink in another corner. Three further doors lead out of this room, one leading up a flight of stone steps to the first floor bedrooms with access straight into the attic. Everywhere you look there's everything you could possibly need to get you through one life, mostly arranged in a way to trip you up. Up another three steps and into a bedroom, which includes a surprisingly bright and modern bathroom, and a door opening out onto the terrace garden with a shallow pond and lots of ferns and rocks and interesting nooks and crannies. Some would say – a lot of potential for a neat and tidy makeover, but I think it's perfect as it is in all its glorious mess. (I wouldn't actually live in it, as there are also snakes living in the rafters). Bob also has a well-stocked *potager* down by the river opposite the house.

A visit from Bob guarantees a huge bunch of fresh flowers, beautifully tied in a bouquet, a bunch of fresh herbs and perhaps a lettuce and some fresh beans – his generosity is quite phenomenal. He lives there from April to October and is a great connoisseur of the countryside and woodland and has a great deal of local knowledge. He helps everyone and is always there when you need him. In his cellar, he appears to have every manner of useful implement, which he happily allows all his friends to borrow. A thoroughly nice and useful chap, and an Aussie, of course.

One chilly October evening, a friend introduced us to the delights of home made *Vin de Noix* (walnut wine) and as we were so enthused about it, she gave us the recipe. As I mentioned before, we had a big walnut tree next to the house, so I listened carefully. Of course she only spoke French, but she said, 'It's very easy, everything's in fours - forty walnuts, four litres of red wine, four something or other of sugar and one litre of *eau de vie*.' Being so intrigued with the *eau de vie* business, I could not remember what the four of the sugar was. Anyway, first to find the eau de vie.

Literally translated, this is 'water of life.' In fact, it is almost 100% proof distilled alcohol made from grapes and the private production of which is quite illegal. However, the secret recipe is handed down the generations in many of these rural families and it is still produced, but to obtain some involves knowing the local Mafia really well. Not realising any of this, we went straight to the nearest village wine co-operative and asked the man for a litre of eau de vie. He looked round furtively making sure there weren't any secret agents from the *Gendarmerie* lurking around, and said 'Come back tomorrow at 7.30 with an empty bottle.' We did. He wasn't there and we never saw him again. So we mentioned this little episode to another friend who said, furtively, 'Come round tomorrow at 7.30 with an empty bottle.' So we did. He disappeared into his cellar and returned shortly with a saucepan full of the stuff. You only had to sniff it from a respectable distance before it made your eyes water. He poured it into our innocuous looking plastic bottle, which we hoped wouldn't melt or, indeed, explode, and we brought it gingerly back to England to make this great walnut wine.

Forty walnuts – no problem. Mixed with four bottles of red wine – no problem. Then the sugar – four what? Couldn't be pounds, they don't use them in France and it couldn't be ounces either. So it must be kilos. Jehan argued about this but as it was a case of the chef always being right, he went along with it. Four kilos of sugar it was – and we stirred and stirred this molasses like mixture, added the eau de vie and left it to do its stuff for – you guessed it – forty days. Like idiots, the grand opening of the first bottle was in France, amongst French friends, including the lady who gave us the recipe. As I poured it out she said "It's quite thick, isn't it" and then we all took a sip. Silence. Then someone said *"C'est tres doux"'* (very sweet), and I said "Well, four kilos of sugar, what do you expect?" At which she exclaimed "Four kilos? I said forty grams!" 'That's the one' I thought, 'Didn't think of grams.' So we laughed a lot about it, poured it all back in the bottle and used it as a superb topping for vanilla ice cream. End of story.

Chapter 13: The Little Dog Laughed to see Such Fun

It was nine o-clock in the evening and still light. We were about to go for a walk. Everything was very still and all you could hear were crickets – rubbing their legs together, I do believe. Apparently, it does wonders for the cricket population. I'm glad I'm not a cricket.

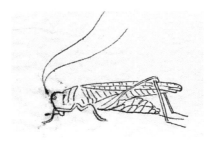

Some of our most entertaining moments have been while attempting to converse in French. As I mentioned earlier, when we first bought our house we spoke school French and were never taught certain useful phrases, or in fact, any useful phrases. After enjoying one of Ginette's wonderful meals – one surprise after another – I was truly full and when she offered me another slice of *tarte aux pommes*, I said *"Merci, je suis plein"* which caused some merriment around the table, but Ginette being the lovely person she is said *"d'accord"* and carried on with the coffee. A few French Linguaphone tapes and several meals later, I discovered that *je suis plein'* (literally, I am full) means 'I am pregnant.' What one should say is *'j'ai assez mangé'* (I have eaten enough). It's just as well to know this now, as there is a need to use this phrase a lot when in France. At a French dinner table, we have learnt to appreciate each dish individually, be it vegetables, potatoes or meat and especially salad. We tend to serve everything up on one plate, but there is joy in tasting each dish on its own – simple green beans cooked with lashings of garlic, fresh thyme and olive oil and crusty bread to wipe the plate with.

Another linguistic hiccup occurred at a restaurant when, being the official French speaker in the family I confidently translated the *plat du jour* as being veal escalopes and chips, which sounded fine. So we ordered four *plats du jour*. It turned out to be boiled liver and potatoes. Well as it happens I like liver, but sadly the rest of the family don't and as a punishment I had to eat a lot of liver. Next time I wasn't so quick to help them, ungrateful lot. I suppose I should be thankful it was liver, and not testicles, which also feature frequently on French menus.

'The Little Dog laughed to see such fun, and the Dish ran away with the Spoon'. This just about describes one of the most enjoyable restaurant meals we've had in France.

It was Bastille Day in Domme, which perches prettily on a hilltop in the Dordogne. We spent three glorious days there in the company of our dear friends, Maggie and Rick. The little dog in question belonged to the chef and has to be given special mention because, throughout the entire evening, he did a little dance swivelling around on his bottom on the doormat – his front paws in a 'begging' position and an ecstatic smirk on his face. Although this added to the charm of the evening in some bizarre way, it was the dinner that was unsurpassable.

The main course was to be cooked on the open fire – our choice of meat cooked to order. So for starters we opted for *une salade,* mentioning that we would like some *salade verte* with the steaks as well. Madame gave us a funny look and shrugged her shoulders as if to say 'if you insist'. Then off she went to fetch the starter salads. They arrived one at a time; a serving dish for each of us, full of all the vegetables you could think of and some fruit as well. In the centre of each platter were slices of pineapple and radiating outwards there were radishes, spring onions, apple, strawberries, red peppers, green peppers, tomatoes, cucumber, asparagus spears, green beans, sweet corn, beetroot, carrots and three kinds of lettuce. Every vegetable was beautifully presented – the colours complimenting each other and the textures contrasting in the most artistic arrangement imaginable. We were speechless as we stared down at this spectacular labour of love before us. There must have been some two pounds of market garden on each dish, all splendidly garnished with bright green parsley, olives, chives and basil, and dressed to perfection.

It really looked too good to eat but there was nothing else for it and we demolished it all, helped along with some excellent wine. We realised now why Madame had given us a strange look when we asked for a salad with our main course. The huge lamb chops and steaks were produced with great ceremony and laid carefully on the grill over the open fire. In spite of just having tucked away the enormous salads, our appetites were being sharpened again as we watched the meat sizzling and took in the divine aroma of sautéed garlic. It was all absolutely delicious and I have no recollection whatsoever of the cheese, the dessert, or indeed, the coffee. By then, the fire, the wine and the dancing dog had most of our attention and the conversation had degenerated to the level that only the best of friends can enjoy. The whole evening was pure magic.

The little dog, I suspect, had a bad case of worms and was actually scratching his itchy bottom on the doormat and having a thoroughly good time, hence the ecstatic smirk on his face. This could only happen in France.

We are slowly discovering that the French will eat almost anything from the animal world and just about every part of it. Nothing goes to waste. I admired someone's vegetable plot one day and remarked on the lack of snails, saying that when I tried to grow lettuce the snails ate them first. To which she said "That's fine, the snails eat the lettuce and you can eat the snails, lucky you!" I still haven't worked out if she was serious, she probably was.

Surely they only eat certain cultivated snails. Snail eating is really such a waste of time – it's not even good if you are on a diet, being as you don't get a lot to eat, because what you do eat is loads of garlic and butter – now that's nice. And bread, to wipe up with, of course.

Having enjoyed so many delicious meals with our French friends, who were typically of the opinion that only the French know about cooking, we decided to throw caution to the wind and invite them all round for an Indian meal followed by that most traditional of Indian deserts – The Sherry Trifle (after all, the British ruled India for over two hundred years). It turned into a big party and for the first time, with many more to follow, we produced a dinner for twelve to fifteen on two camping gas burners and no oven. It was a 'bring your own chairs, plates and cutlery' – great fun.

The spices for the chicken curry were blended with caution as this was probably the first time our provincial friends were being introduced to such thoroughly foreign food, all washed down with gallons of wine. All the dishes were greatly appreciated, but the most successful was the Sherry Trifle. Jelly is not easily available in rural France, and the French selection of desserts is usually limited to crème caramel, a tart of some description, chocolate *soufflé* or an *île flottante.* Yes, well! Now, were we living in Paris it might be different, but this is the Aveyron – no fancy stuff - just basic regional cooking. So the evening passed in a haze of exotic spices and songs, to the sound of the accordion, in the light of our beautiful kerosene lamps.

Walking our guests back to their cars on a dark night fortified by vast quantities of good wine was a fun operation. Everyone had to leave together, as the lamps and torches went in procession down the stone steps to the stream, across the bridge and up the steep drive. You could, of course, make as much noise as you wish, as there were no neighbours. Actually, you could not see another house from ours. Honest. On a clear July night all you saw were stars – no lights, no pollution. One night we saw shooting stars continuously – entire worlds disappearing. It puts life into perspective, forcing you to consider what really matters. How necessary is all the stress we put ourselves through? Should we allow other people and events to irritate and upset us as much as they do? Of course not. We all finish up like the shooting stars in the end.

This brings us to our first encounter with Oysters. One September, driving from Calais to Angouleme, we broke our journey at Claix to visit Jeromine and Erick and their newborn baby, Mahaut. We checked in at a nearby hotel before meeting them for an evening meal. Her in-laws were visiting them too, and as this would, most likely, be a huge French dinner, we hadn't eaten much that day, having travelled a long way. Well, we duly rang them at 6 pm from the telephone box in the village having followed their directions over the tiny bridge which went over the tiny river shaded by huge oak trees protecting this quiet place and hiding it from the outside world.

Erick appeared as if by magic in his little red car out of the vineyards which stretched for miles in every direction, these being the grapes that produce that elixir of life, Cognac. After much kissing and hand shaking we followed Erick through the vineyards and up the hill into deep and leafy woods. The road was a narrow track, which wound this way and that and finally arrived at a clearing with four or five houses, newly built, each with its own large garden. They were still in the process of tiling the floors and putting the finishing touches on their house.

An old wooden table with a bright plastic tablecloth stood ready with an assortment of glasses and bottles of aperitifs. After further kissing and hand shaking and much admiration of the baby who was, naturally, truly beautiful, we sat down with a drink, looking forward to our eagerly awaited French dinner. Several drinks later we were given a tour of the house – I could see no sign of food in the half built kitchen and a slight panic was beginning to descend – helped along by all the alcohol on empty stomachs. Then Erick announced 'we're having a barbecue!' So - spirits rose again (quite literally) as another round of drinks was served in anticipation. The sun was setting by this time so dinner was surely not far away but there was no sign of the barbecue.

Eventually, Erick's mother arrived with a basket of runner beans and another of potatoes and sat down to top and tail the beans. We resigned ourselves to our fate and offered to help in the hope of speeding the process. While we peeled and chopped, Erick fetched an axe to cut wood for the barbecue – none of your modern gas fired contraptions here in this rural idyll. Experience has taught us that basic barbecues take a very long time to heat up sufficiently to cook upon, so when offered the choice 'Would you like fish or meat?' we promptly said 'Fish' thinking it would be marginally quicker.

At last, we all went indoors to set the table, carrying our garden chairs in with us. Completely woozy with drink, any sort of food was going to be welcome, but the climax came when, with a great flourish, two enormous platters of oysters arrived at the table. Raw oysters – on the very first night of our holiday. Jehan is not at all keen on shellfish at the best of times, but manners got the better of us and we swallowed the first slurpy mouthful, holding our breath and gritting our teeth (this being quite tricky to do while swallowing oysters). With a huge squeeze of lemon or shallots in vinegar they were reasonably palatable. This was a learning curve for us. Apparently, oysters like wine, have a different flavour depending on where they are from and a connoisseur is able to identify the origin from the taste and texture. Had we not been so hungry I doubt if we could have devoured as many as we did, washed down with yet more wine. Following the oysters there was fish steamed in foil with tomatoes and the french beans – (now cooked with olive oil and garlic) and the potatoes – fried to perfection. Erick meanwhile was still messing around with the barbecue, which was making lots of smoke and no fire. Had this been England it would have rained just as he got it going.

The most wonderful part of the entire meal was the atmosphere in which it was enjoyed. Everyone was so relaxed and the baby didn't cry even once. She slept and had a feed and slept again in a little basket on the floor – no fuss, no bother. They made us so welcome and so happy that it felt as if we had been there for ages (we had, really, waiting for dinner). For dessert, a punnet of peaches arrived on the table. We were really stuffed to the limit by now but Josanne insisted on our tasting them. They were 'blood peaches', with red flesh and from the local orchard and also the best peaches I have ever tasted – really, really delicious. We have not been able to find these red-fleshed peaches anywhere else – only white or yellow. So the evening was stamped on our memories forever.

The next morning, continuing on our journey eastwards, cross country through the

Dordogne towards the Aveyron, not far from Claix on the D5 towards Villebors-Lavalette, we saw a sign for 'Chateau de la Mercerie' to the left. It looked intriguing, as the road it pointed to was mysterious and leafy, so off we went, winding gently uphill.

Then we saw it – just a glimpse at first of white pillars and arches – hidden among the trees. On drawing closer, the full splendour of this chateau became apparent. White marble throughout, a series of graceful arches rising above a high marble plinth like some fairy-tale ballroom without a ceiling. Ivy clung to the pillars of this long forgotten palace in a dream. The main building with its intricately carved decoration was also sheer white marble and had its huge French windows on the first floor hauntingly half open, giving us glimpses of the sumptuous interior. The chateau was clearly being lived in as there were notices all around warning us that this was a private estate. Was Sleeping Beauty still in there, we wondered, waiting for her Prince Charming to kiss the palace awake? We gazed at the fantasy in awe and then left it to sleep for another hundred years.

Chapter 14: Boutique Rukshana

In 1996, Jehan took early retirement from the bank as twenty-six years of shift work was taking its toll. As I had always fancied the idea of owning a boutique, which would be a showcase for my designs, we decided to rent a lovely shop in the village. With great excitement we named the shop 'Rukshana' and it was opened by the then Mayor of Elmbridge, Councillor Hugh Ashton. Every garment was designed and made by me. I made pure silk jackets and dresses in lovely bright colours, combining texture and design, and the results were unique, but very wearable. The opening night was most encouraging and the shop quickly became very popular.

103 Hare lane, Claygate   1996 to 2014

My intention was to 1) Take an order, 2) Give a fitting the following week, and 3) Have the outfit ready the week following. Well – the orders that flooded in proved that: 1) Everyone loved my designs and 2) I couldn't cope! So we started buying in a few ready-mades. I soon realised that this was a much easier option and have never looked back. I still took orders for wedding gowns, bridesmaids dresses and spectacular patchwork silk evening jackets and worked like there was no tomorrow, often late into the night. The fashion shows still took place every year but I began including unusual and top quality designer labels that we discovered at the various Fashion trade shows we attended.

Scouting had to go in 1998 as it all got a bit too much. I was reluctant to leave as leaders are so hard to come by and I enjoyed it so much, but a friend suggested I think of a bucket of water and myself as a stick stirring the water. When the stick is withdrawn the water returns to its original state till somebody else comes along to stir it. Amazingly, this is just what happened, and I left my Cub Pack in very good hands.

The shop became an integral part of Claygate and a sort of 'Village Well' where everyone came to 1) say hello, 2) complain about all and sundry, 3) ask advice on health matters and tips on losing weight and, 4) buy quality clothing, usually in that order! Still, every year was profitable and most enjoyable. I have made some lovely friends especially among the ladies who modelled in our annual fund raising fashion shows. Running the shop has also provided me with plenty of hilarious stories about customers and their peculiarities, which will make a brilliant subject matter for a book in the future! After forty-five years in the dress business there isn't much I don't know about the strange things that happen to the female figure as it ages disgracefully. The secret of success is finding the right cut and design of clothing for particular shape problems and there is great pleasure in sending a client on her way feeling beautiful and confident in what she is wearing.

Two years after opening the shop, we had a surprise. Daraius, (then twenty-two), announced that he would like to get married to Becky, (then eighteen and still at university), that same year. In these days of couples living together before making that decision, we were taken aback but also impressed that they knew their minds. It was no good saying that they wouldn't find a venue at this late stage. They liked the idea of a large marquee in our back garden and they had already booked the church and also spoken to the vicar! The date, we were informed, was the 22nd of August. There is nothing like having a very short time to organise a wedding. It does away with thinking too much about it and endless arguments about finite details.

To my joy, Becky asked me to make her wedding dress (she wouldn't have dared to ask anyone else), and the dresses for her three sisters, who would be the bridesmaids. We had a wonderful excuse to nip over to France to buy the champagne! Becky's parents organised a wonderful lunch and the flowers to decorate the church and the marquee. The marquee arrived the day before, and covered the entire garden. The evening before, we decorated it with florist's ribbon in peach and cream. The kitchen was cleared and cleaned thoroughly to accommodate the caterers, who would arrive early the following morning. Feroza and Andrea had come down from Italy a couple of days earlier. The day dawned bright and clear, and in all the excitement going on, Daraius announced that he needed to have a haircut. So, without much ado, Jehan sat him down at the bottom of the garden and gave him a haircut!

They were married at Christchurch, in Esher, by a lady vicar who was delightful and relaxed. So relaxed, in fact, that she had forgotten to bring their marriage certificates with her. Our friend John was commandeered halfway through his video–ing of the wedding ceremony to nip back to Claygate and fetch them. That is why we have complete coverage of the beginning and the end of the nuptials but a gap in the middle. She gave a lovely sermon, in which she likened a happy marriage to a roll of Andrex toilet paper, for which the advertising slogan was 'Soft, Strong and very Long', which was amusing and very true.

It really was a lovely, warm and beautiful day. Never having been involved with a church wedding, we left all the important stuff to Becky's parents, so, as far as I am concerned, it was extremely easy! Having been involved with making wedding dresses for so many years, I would hear many horror stories about things going wrong before or during the wedding. None of this happened for us. It was also the right decision for them to marry when they did, because four years later, we became very young and proud grandparents! They will be coming up for their eighteenth wedding anniversary soon!

Quite apart from running the shop, we also joined the Claygate Village Association. As ever, we went in head first and it took over our lives. At one stage, Jehan took over as the Secretary. He also became a Parish Councillor for Claygate and a Trustee of the Claygate Village Hall. Anyone who is a member of a Village committee has to be greatly respected. There are not many people who are altruistic enough to give their time and energy for the benefit of others in their community. We were proud to be part of a team that organised the Christmas Lights events, Open Garden Trails and above all, the Claygate Music Festival.

We had several musical friends, and each year, when the children were younger, we held a musical soirée at home, at which everyone performed their party piece, be it poetry or music. My particular party piece was alter-ego Madame

Fifi, who was a feisty but ageing blonde who played the accordion and sang French songs rather badly (well, so did Edith Piaf). A lady of the night who was now too long in the tooth to be profitably desirable, she came about when I discovered a manky blond wig left over from one of the Scout Gang shows. I also found a black beret and some dark sunglasses Red fishnet tights, high heeled boots, basque and frilly skirt followed. Madame Fifi made her public debut at the first Music Festival as part of the Old Time Music Hall event. A gentleman I'd known for several years asked his wife – "What's the French lady got to do with it?" The disguise clearly worked well!

Madame Fifi

These music evenings, with all the local talent around, gave us the idea for a Claygate Music Festival, perhaps a long weekend of variety performances in the village. Well, this turned into a two week long Extravaganza, with all genres of music performed by professionals and amateurs, children and grown-ups. It was Rock to Baroque. Everyone wanted to be part of it. Holy Trinity Church and Claygate Village Hall became the main venues, with the Community Centre and the Christian Science Church hosting events too. There were wonderful volunteers who came forward to help with setting up chairs, refreshments and publicity. It was a marathon to organise, but what a resounding success it was. Most of the performers had a village connection, which made it all the more special. Our younger son, Jamsheed, was by now a highly professional piano entertainer and gave a hugely popular concert as part of the Festival. The 1st Claygate Scout and Guide Band was, by this time under the leadership of Robin Wilkinson, and going from strength to strength. They are performing for the Queen at Windsor Castle this year, and have also led the Eurodisney New Year's Day Parade, in Paris.

Following the success of the first attempt, there was a Claygate Music Festival held every two years. Five Festivals and almost ten years later, we have handed it over to someone else to organise, having printed out a sheet on 'How to organise a Music Festival in 10 easy steps'. It will be interesting to see what direction someone new will steer it in.

Chapter 15: Carcassone, Cathars and the Helicopter

Carcassonne

To equip the house with bits and bobs, we frequently visited a wonderful store called Brad Centre. It was a huge place that stocked just about everything you could possibly need – from saucepans to bed linen, battery-operated gadgets to wellington boots, water pumps, airguns and garden tools. The kind of shop one needs when attempting to set up home on a shoestring. After a while, we got to know the staff pretty well, especially a very pleasant lady at the till. She seemed to be the friendliest and most efficient salesperson there, apart from the tall, strong man who heaved our huge concrete planter into the VW camper. (Unloading it at the other end was quite another story).

While paying for our purchases one day, we mentioned to *Madame* that we were planning a trip to Carcassone. She got quite animated, as that was her home town, and gave us a detailed history of the area. Then she said, "The next time you visit Millau, you must come to dinner." We said we'd love to – maybe later that year in July. I have to add that at this stage, our command of conversational French was still shaky. Sure enough, as soon as we arrived that summer at Brad Centre for our holiday fix of shopping, she greeted us warmly and invited us for dinner on the following Friday evening.

We accepted happily, assuming all the time that she was one of the workers there and lived in a tiny flat, somewhere in the overdeveloped part of Millau. She also said, "Bring your swimming costumes if you like – it's going to be hot." So then we assumed she lived by the river, where most people went for a dip – (well, we did, anyway). When we asked *"Où est votre maison?"* she handed us a card with the name on it and gave us rather easy instructions like "Follow the signs for the Chateau" to which we said, "Okay'" and assumed she lived in a tiny flat, by the river, on the way to the Chateau. So you're with me so far. Yes, you guessed it – when we read the name properly, we realised it was the same name in letters six feet high on the huge DIY store next door which had branches in several big towns all over France. And yes, they did live in the Chateau – that was just one of their residences. So we went to dinner at 8 p.m. on Friday.

Jamsheed was with us, as Daraius being of the age when he would rather wreak havoc at home in England, with a few wild parties, than come with us on holiday. Well, as long as he was enjoying himself too.

As we drove up to the gates, they swung open automatically to let us in. This was a beautiful old Roman Villa with the addition of a huge conservatory and an Olympic size swimming pool (not quite the river), with an outdoor kitchen and barbecue area and changing rooms at one end. A bottle of champagne lay cooling in a silver bucket with a dish of caviar and snowy white napkins beside it. It was like a Hollywood film set and completely unlike anything we'd been expecting. We ate by the pool at a beautiful glass dining table with green wrought iron legs, which of course matched the chairs, which matched the coffee table, which matched the small tables – colour co-ordinated everything. Even the colours of the patio containers matched the décor.

The garden also included a well-stocked vegetable plot. Genevieve was an accomplished lady, obviously very clever and artistic. Her husband Michel, the tall strong man working hard at the shop, was equally friendly and warm hearted. Many years of friendship have passed since then and we still wonder why she suddenly decided to invite us, total strangers who spoke rather bad French, into her beautiful home with such trust and open hearted generosity.

There must be some truth in the old theory of vibrations. When I was little, my favourite uncle had written in my autograph book 'You can fool some of the people all of the time and all of the people some of the time, but you can't fool all of the people all of the time.' A latter day translation could be ' You can be on the same wave length as some people all of the time and never be on the same wave length as some other people all of the time – only some of the time.' This could be the reason that we instantly like some people and would rather keep our distance from others. Now I've given you some deep thinking to do. Or, you can just leave it there. But there's definitely something in the ether that makes things happen.

Anyway, back to the lovely meal. It was very simple – the most exquisite piece of melon, a 'melt in your mouth' piece of fillet steak, potatoes *dauphinois*, fine *haricots vert* (in season from her garden), a beautiful fresh salad also from the *potager* and a fresh peach sorbet. Oh, and it all started with the bottle of champagne. I had the gall to say I didn't drink white wine, including champagne as it triggered off cramps, so could I have the red instead; in spite of which they carried on being nice to us. Genevieve's French was very easy for us to understand as she spoke clearly and I suspect she also spoke a little English so could choose her words carefully for us to follow. It was a superb evening and a grand surprise.

Taking the bull by the horns the following summer we invited them to Joumeyrac. We warned them about wearing sensible shoes and not bringing the car down the drive, not realising at the time that Michel had actually spent his childhood here in Roquetaillade. He used to catch *ecrevisse* (crayfish) in our little stream. There was a lot more water in it then. It had since been diverted at the top to water the *potagers* of Montjaux, so we got what was left, which was usually enough for us. Our stream was called the Matazou, which flows into the Muse, which joins the Tarn, which joins the Lot and they all flow together into the Garonne, which flows into the Atlantic ocean. There you have it. From little streams mighty rivers do grow.

It was a relaxed and cosy evening at Joumeyrac. Dinner was *à l'Indienne* with salad and bread added of course, and cheese before dessert. We lit our lovely kerosene lamps with the mantles and walked our friends back to their car in the starlight at midnight. For them it was as unusual an evening as ours had been at their house the first time. We have always invited them to England but they have yet to take up the offer. The last time they were in England, they went on a full scale foxhunt so you can guess what sort of hospitality that included. Never mind, everyone's different!

Going back to Genevieve's hometown of Carcassone - this is one of the most beautifully restored and picturesque medieval fortresses in

France. A lot of renovation and rebuilding has been done, to the dismay of orthodox medieval scholars, but to the common man it is a fairytale fortress with many turrets and flags, many miles of ramparts and within the walls, the most interesting craft shops ever. A genuine tourist trap if ever there was one. It has been used as a backdrop to many a Hollywood Blockbuster, including the film Robin of Sherwood.

There is always something going on in Carcassone. One year there was a Jazz concert – quite incongruous considering the surroundings, and although it was absolutely first class, what we remember most is the French chanteuse singing 'Stormy weather' that lovely song made famous by Ella Fitzgerald. The last line goes 'it's raining all the time' but it sounded like 'it's running all the time' and it was one of those silly moments when we thought this was hugely funny and laughed about it for days. One would think there wasn't enough amusement in our lives. What's worse, we still laugh about it.

Every year Carcassone held a jousting event, with superb horsemen doing their trick displays. How they managed to control their horses in such a confined space, at full gallop, was impressive. They were The Horsemen of the Camargue, skilled in training wild horses and completely in tune with their animals. We all cheered for the white knight and booed the black knight, who really upset the children – poor man – he was only doing his job. Life in Carcassone in the middle ages must have been very hard, just as it was everywhere else. Even the richest nobility living in the grandest chateaux had to cope with freezing cold winters in those huge rooms, wearing layers of clothing which were removed probably once a month for a good wash. With such a total lack of hygiene it's no wonder they were all bad tempered and at each other's throats all the time.

The region west and south of Carcassonne was the stronghold of the Cathar movement. During the mid-12th century, the Catholic Church reigned supreme, with the priests being all powerful, increasingly wealthy and thoroughly corrupt. The Cathar concept was that all material things were evil and only a pure spiritual existence was the ideal. In pursuit of this spiritual purity they practised celibacy, wore plain black robes, lived on the charity of others and did not eat any food that resulted from sexual union, which included eggs, milk and meat. Having 'perfected' themselves to their satisfaction they then starved themselves to death: all very impressive but no fun whatsoever. The movement grew in popularity, as it clearly denounced the corruption and materialism of the then Catholic Church, encouraging its followers not to pay taxes and tithes to the Bishops.

The first major fracas with the Catholic authorities broke out in Albi, followed by much bloodshed, as Simon de Montfort took charge of sweeping away the Cathars. 1209 to 1245 was yet another turbulent period of religious warfare. The Cathar martyrs died in their thousands and plenty of ordinary people too, as was the case in Beziers in 1209 when the Albigensian crusaders (mercenaries who were promised entry to heaven for 40 days crusading) wiped out the entire population just to make sure they did not miss any Cathars. However, the cleverer ones who saw what was coming escaped in advance to the country, so the whole exercise was ruthlessly pointless. It's absolutely true that the love of money is the root of most evil – and that religion is the cause of much anguish and bloodshed. Even a firm Cathar believer might have renounced his faith for a few million francs.........

Exploring in the Pyrenees, we came across some intriguing happenings on the river Hers where it emerges from its underground passage. The place is called La Fontaine de Fontestorbes. Due to some unusual rock alignment deep inside the mountain, the river periodically stops flowing for a few minutes; a stretch of riverbed draining away, and becoming dry enough to cross over into the mouth of the cave. After a quick and daring dash into the cave, you hear the rumble of water welling up deep inside the mountain, and in great excitement, rush back to the safety of the bank as a furious swell gushes out, frothing and bubbling. Then it settles down and quietly drains away to a mere trickle before the fun starts again. This has been going on for many years and causes huge amusement. There might, quite possibly, be a little man who turns a tap on and off inside the mountain – or maybe the Devil playing tricks again, but then again, possibly not.

Due east from Fontestorbes are the deep and singularly spectacular Gorges de Galamus. The road is narrow and perilously steep, winding alongside the gorge, which is half a kilometre deep in some parts. The water down below is green and icy cold. There are few places to stop, but we found one, and the boys discovered a swimming hole. This looked like an exceptionally deep pool. It was crystal clear, reflecting the overhanging rocks and cliffs. We watched other youngsters cheerfully jumping off the rocks into the water to cool off, and as nobody drowned or did themselves any major injury in the space of ten minutes, our boys decided to jump in – fully clothed, for some strange reason, which seemed a good idea at the time. They had a wonderful afternoon, as it was the height of summer and the water was delightfully cold. We tied their wet clothes to the roof rack to dry off on the way back and carried on up the gorges, enjoying the most superb views of rock worn smooth by swirling water over millions of years. The fact that the French have made a perfectly serviceable road around the top of this gorge is very creditable and is a feat of construction, as space is very limited due to the sheer cliffs on both sides of the gorge.

There are many spectacular Cathar fortresses, all of which are within smoke signalling distance of each other. One of the most impressive of these is Peyrepertuse, further up from the Galamus. The walls are actually built into the rock face on top of a high mountain and it's difficult to differentiate between rock and wall.

Peyrepertuse

One might even mistake the whole thing for a jagged rock formation. It is very big and very forbidding and must have been a truly bleak place in its heyday. Again, I feel so sad that people had to resort to protecting themselves within structures like these because of a lack of tolerance for different beliefs.

The most difficult fortress to reach is Montsegur, which has only one very narrow and steep walking pathway to it – very dangerous in wet weather and not so easy in the dry, as the natural stone steps have been worn very smooth over the centuries and are extremely slippery. There are no barriers and no railings. We climbed up to the very top, with total disregard for health and safety, being overtaken now and again by very elderly, and obviously much fitter, locals. How the Cathars got their food, animals and supplies up and down is mind-boggling. At least no double-glazing salesmen or Jehovah's Witnesses came to call, (or was it before their day). Now, that has to be a plus point.

The reason for the limited access was obvious. They could easily hide the pathway and stop the enemy coming up. Montsegur was one of the last hideouts for the persecuted Cathars, and on a mountaintop opposite, the army of the Church constructed a huge catapult with which they bombarded Montsegur. Really, a lot of effort. Eventually, after being under continuous siege for nearly a year, Montsegur surrendered, but at a great cost. All the Cathars were given the choice of renouncing their faith or throwing themselves into the flames of an enormous fire in the field below. Hundreds martyred themselves for the sake of their belief. There is a sad little plaque there to mark the massacre of 1244. Such a waste of life but this is the stuff our history is made of. How humanity ever progressed to CD players, computers, satellite television and trips to the moon after all that, is mystifying.

When mankind stops fighting over religion there may be some movement towards true civilization. How so many different intelligent human beings can be convinced about so many different ideas, none of which can ever be proven, and then run their lives on pure faith in the unknown, is a constant enigma. We are never going to know where we came from or why we are here. Nor will we ever know where we go afterwards, so why not make the most of what we've got, making others happy and thereby making ourselves happy – enjoy life while you can. Think about it – most of the troubles in the world really are due to religious wars – people destroy their own lives and others, in pursuit of something nobody really knows about. Not much has changed since the Middle Ages in that respect, except that we have a super efficient media service now. In those days news took a long time to travel – I guess smoke signals were pretty trendy. Of course there are natural disasters, disabilities and all manner of problems that cannot be avoided; and for those I feel great sorrow, but if religious arguments could be ended how much better life would be. Enough theosophy – now for the helicopter story.

One fine day, we decided to pay a second visit to the fortress of Quéribus, (within smoke signalling distance of Peyrepertuse), which sits atop a hill. It is quite ruined now, but the *donjon* is in good condition and the view from the top is breathtaking. Looking across the broad valley to the chain of the Pyrenees one can see the majestic peak of Pic du Canigou (2784 m). From a previous visit we knew that there was a huge car park at the top of the hill next to the *Chateau*. However, this time we arrived to find lots of cars parked at the bottom of the hill, so we naturally assumed that the top car park was full. I say 'we' but only 'I' assumed that. Jehan, being the type who has to try everything, said 'Just because everyone is parked down here, doesn't mean there's no place on top. Let's go and see.'

So, onwards and upwards we drove, following closely behind an army truck and followed by another army truck, both full of soldiers, not that we thought that this was anything unusual. The fact that one smart soldier actually saluted us and waved us on was also nothing remarkable. After all, this was France and the French army displays itself on manoeuvres everywhere.

Arriving at the summit, we were saluted again and found the car park completely empty except for some army activity. Jehan, as smug as a bug said, "See - plenty of space!" Choosing a particularly good spot and switching off the engine we thought we might stop for a while to see what these soldiers were up to. Rolling the windows down, we took out our sandwiches and settled back. Five minutes passed – nobody took much notice of us. Then, suddenly, one soldier got up and started waving his arms frantically, shouting " *Allez y! No Parking ici!* " It took a few moments to realise that he was yelling at us, by which time several young men were waving their arms in a great panic and screaming "NO PARKING! NO PARKING!" Then we heard a whirring sound and Jamsheed said in a very calm but shaky voice "Dad, I think a helicopter wants to land on us" – and sure enough – behind us a huge army helicopter had appeared over the rim of the mountain as if from nowhere. I've never seen Jehan start the car so quickly and shoot out of the way.

The helicopter landed briefly on the exact spot the car had been and several soldiers somersaulted out of it and rolled off into the bushes. An army exercise – a surprise attack on Quéribus. We realised then that the pilot was probably also a trainee – imagine his horror at finding this car with an English number plate, parked precisely where he had to land – his arrival was supposed to be secret and perfect. In fact it was so secret, nobody even told us. Can you imagine an army exercise like this being organised in England? It would have been in the papers and there would have been huge notices all over the place to keep the public away, instead of which they actually saluted us and waved us through. There were no flags on our car, nor were we in uniform.

We spent the rest of the morning shaking and sitting in the car at a very safe distance, too embarrassed to cross army lines and visit Quéribus. When they had all gone home (*naturellement* they abandoned the siege at 12 noon for lunch) we continued with our visit. Laughing about this incident then, we still laugh about it now, but give or take a couple of seconds it could have made the BBC news as a major disaster. Fortunately I'm still here to tell the tale. Several times over.

Chateau de Quéribus

Chapter 16: The Wonderful Gorges du Tarn

Follow the river Tarn upstream through Millau and you will eventually arrive at the spectacularly impressive Gorges du Tarn. The approach is gentle enough, past the historic old village of Compeyre perched up on a hill to your left and the river flowing peacefully on your right, flanked by wide grassy banks and fruit orchards. Gradually, the road starts to climb and after Rivière sur Tarn the road gets higher and the valley gets deeper on the right. The mountains on your left rise loftier and craggier, and high above is the ruined castle of Peyrellade, a majestic relic of the feudal past when sections of the river were owned by different lords, all of whom, *normallement,* fought with each other most of the time. The view is stupendous in every direction.

In certain places, the road has been carved out of the mountain and there are natural stone archways spanning the road, which is narrow with tortuous bends. All this makes for exciting driving, especially in the high tourist season with international coaches bringing hordes of visitors to admire the gorges. Add to this the Dutch caravaners and the German Hymermobiles, and there is little hope for the polite British driver who prefers the wrong side of the road anyway. It's a nightmare in the high season, but so beautiful that it is worth it.

Across the river to your right a little further on, is a tiny village clinging to the mountainside, access to which is from this side of the river – by boat. All quite feasible in summer when the water level is very low but impossible after the winter rains, when the Tarn is in full flood. There are several places at which to stop and admire the view and just enough cafés at strategic points. Everywhere you look there are weird stone formations, windswept rocks that change their appearance at every angle, looming high above you in awesome splendour. In places the valley drops to 1500 feet and you cannot see the river at all. This is a river canyon in its truest sense, carved out over millions of years; proof that our Earth does its own thing regardless of man's activities and his efforts to tame it. When the snows melt on the Cevennes mountains, this river is a mighty torrent sweeping trees and anything in its path downstream, bursting its banks and breaking bridges in its fury. After which, it settles down happily and gives great joy to all the holidaymakers who come to canoe down it and picnic in the gorge.

One memorable day, we set off to canoe down the Tarn with our friends Therese, her three daughters, Stefanie, Jeromine, and Geraldine, one of their boyfriends and his dog (a daft and friendly pitbull terrier called Hercules), and our family. Arriving at La Malene, we hired some canoes, put all our valuables into watertight cylinders, donned our lifejackets and off we went. The river in summer is absolutely perfect for 'Canoeing for beginners' – shallow enough in most parts with a few fast flowing rapids to make it mildly exciting. It was a beautiful day and we felt very small in this majestic place with sheer rock walls on both sides and the clear water sparkling all around us.

We set off with great excitement, dog and all. The sun was scorching, the water was cool and fresh, and the huge overhangs of rock under which we passed in our canoes were covered in moss and ferns where they never saw the sunlight. Everywhere you looked there was something wonderful to see, and above us Earth's very own skyscrapers, closing in on you as they do in New York. We stopped along the way at any inviting looking spots for a swim, pulling the canoes onto a sandy bank for a picnic. There were hundreds of trout in the river - there for the tickling.

Most of us were sharing double canoes, but Jamsheed had decided to take a kayak by himself. The stretch of river we were on had one or two pockets of swirling water – mini whirlpools that are best avoided specially in the small kayaks, which capsize very easily. Needless to say, Jamsheed capsized and it was a moment of sheer panic for us when he did not resurface for a while. I kept thinking ' someone, turn the water off!' When he did eventually reappear, having lost his sunglasses, his dignity and the kayak (which popped up further downstream) it brought home the fact that all nature's elements are to be respected and never taken for granted. With a great sense of relief and joy, we thoroughly enjoyed the rest of the day and it was the first of many more trips down the Tarn.

There is fun to be had in the Gorges du Tarn for everyone, regardless of age or ability.

The more intrepid canoeists can do a run of over 25 km. starting from St Enimie further up the river, negotiating several rapids and deeper stretches of water and paddling all the way down past La Malene to the finishing point just before Les Vignes. Here, the canoes are collected by the hire company and everyone rides back up to the starting point in the minibus. There is no time limit as the transporters ply continuously up and down and one can enjoy several picnics and swims on the way.

For the less athletic, the shorter trip from La Malene is recommended – less effort and even more time for picnics. For them as can't be bothered to paddle or get wet, there are flat-bottomed boats manned by expert handlers to take you down the river. These have apparently been in existence since at least the last century as they are mentioned in a couple of old books. They are called *Barques* and used to be poled by the boatmen, like gondolas. They are now motorised and probably sleeker, though not quite as romantic. For anyone remaining who doesn't like the water, there are pebbly stretches of beach to set up your easel and paint or simply read a book – though it would be a shame to bury yourself in a book with all this beauty around you.

All kinds of people converge on the Tarn. Once, we even saw a Hindu mystic submerge himself in the water with his hands folded in prayer and holding his breath under water long enough to make us think he had departed to his spiritual home.

To the east of the Gorges du Tarn lies the Causse Mejean, a vast area of limestone rock riddled with spectacular grottoes and caverns. Driving along this barren landscape, wild and dry with outcrops of rock and yellow grass, one cannot imagine the wonders that exist far below the ground. One of the most impressive of these underground caverns is Aven Armand.

A cable lift takes you down and as you leave daylight behind to enter into the earth, you suddenly realise just how much more there is to learn. In our daily lives, the sky is usually visible no matter where you are, always reminding you of your own insignificance, but this subterranean world of mystery and shadows, dripping and still growing, is something else. There are hundreds of stone steps to enable you to reach vantage points along the way to see the wonderful and weird stone sculptures that have been formed by stalagmites and stalactites – yes, the 'tites' drip down to form the 'mites' often uniting to form pillars of strange shapes and huge proportions. Some of the most remarkable features are floodlit. They have been named, but each person appreciates beauty in a different way, so you interpret them as you please and, no doubt, in ten years time they will be different. The largest cavern is higher and wider than any concert hall that I have seen and indeed, in the summer months it is used for musical events.

We had the good fortune to be here for one of these performances. A good choir, singing in these surroundings, would be fantastic with the acoustics and atmosphere. But alas, it was not our luckiest day – we were to be entertained by a brass band. The sublime and the ridiculous rolled into one. Not that I have anything against brass bands mind you, I really love them, but not in these circumstances. However, brass and hearty percussion it was, sitting on damp chairs being dripped on gently all the time, but it was fun. One day we will return to hear the Slaves Chorus from Nabucco performed here. That will be perfect.

Strange formations at Aven Armand

To share the magic of the gorges, we took our close friends Maggie and Rick on a wet picnic in the canoes. They were staying at a holiday *gite* near Rodez and had come over to spend a night with us at Joumeyrac. They had been pre-warned that they would be sharing our bedroom and using a bathroom in a *cave* with wild animals and, considering Maggie drove a BMW convertible and Rick didn't go anywhere without the latest technological equipment (all of it), they did remarkably well. I think the whole experience was a bit of a blur, helped along by our favourite St. Saturnin wine. The day we went canoeing, I smartly got everything wet and had forgotten to bring any dry underwear, with the result that Rick chivalrously lent me a pair of his underpants. I did say he has all the necessary equipment (and spares) with him at all times. It makes a good after-dinner story.

Chapter 17: Soirée Saucisson

All our summer visitors were treated to a visit to the gorge. Mary, Ken and their young son Thomas were no exception, so on a sunny bright summer morning we packed a picnic and set off, intending to hire canoes and have a lovely lazy day. Arriving at the river we went down to inspect the water level. Suddenly, there was a huge flash of lightning, followed by the most enormous crash of thunder. The sky became darker and darker and there we were, surrounded by these sheer walls of rock bouncing the thunder back and forth. It was truly impressive and not a little bit scary. We ran back to the camper, as huge drops of rain began to fall, threw ourselves in and watched the rain come down in sheets like Noah's flood. That was the end of the picnic. On our way home, the sun came out and it turned into a beautiful evening.

A ruined castle on top of a stone outcrop in the Gorges

The next morning, a gentleman from Roquetaillade came up to our house to invite us to join in the *'soirée saucisson'* in the village that Saturday. When we told him that we had some English friends with us, he said, 'The more the merrier' so we all went to the *soirée*. The dinner was lovely – Bangers and mash and cabbage, but romantically French *'saucisson, pommes de terre et choucroute'* and plenty of *vin ordinaire.* 'Le disco' consisted of somebody's tape recorder in the back of an estate car, but the dance floor was hot stuff.

Roquetaillade has a concrete dance floor in the car park, especially constructed for such social occasions. How about that? No café, shops or telephone box but a dance floor. So we danced the night away.

Little Thomas (Tom) did not speak any French and little Marine (Ginette's granddaughter), spoke no English. She was 10 and he was 7. She wanted to ask him to dance, so she came and asked me how to say, *'Voulez-vous danser avec moi ?'* in English – so I said 'Will you dance with me.' Five little words – but for a 10 year old in a foreign language it was truly difficult. She began 'Weezu denz wizmi' or something to that effect. We tried several times and she finally thought she'd mastered it. She ran off to Tom and said 'Tomas !' and he said 'Huh ?' 'Tomas, weezu .....weezu....' came running back to me, saying ' *j'ai oubliée'* (I've forgotten). So we started all over again, 'will you dance with me' etc. This went on for a long and very painful 10 minutes till, finally, 'Tomas!' 'Huh ?' *'Weezu danz wiz mee ?'* and the answer ? 'No.' Men! I ask you. So that was that. She taught him to count to ten in French instead.

Tom had a special ball that he had brought to play with. It was a new toy and was quickly eyed up by one of the local children, a little boy of three, called Leo. Tom gave it to him to play with. The little boy promptly lost it and there were tears all round. Then a little dog arrived on the scene with the ball in his mouth – everyone happy – and Tom, bless his generous heart, gave the ball to the little boy as a present. May he always be like that.

Leo lives in a caravan with his parents as his mother inherited a barn, which they are in the process of converting into a house for themselves. Six years on and the barn is still undergoing renovation. It's a long story but you are going to hear it!

The barn is situated on a bend in the road coming out of Roquetaillade towards our place – not within view of our house, but in quite a prominent position. It was a perfectly sound building to start with, but had a few little problems with damp in the basement. To alleviate this problem, Leo's father decided to cut away some of the rock behind the barn, to separate it from the mountainside into which it was built. Big mistake. He hit a major underground water source and then had to cut away about a hundred square metres of rock to detach the building from the water source, so it was from the frying pan into the fire, and we are talking about solid granite rock and tons of it.

Now, this enormous excavation of rock had to go somewhere. There would be at least twenty lorry loads of it – beautiful solid stone in lovely colours and unusual shapes where it had split, but where to put it? Well, the bridge at Roquetaillade is too delicate for a lorry full of heavy rocks to be driven over it towards the proper dumping ground – so – up the hill it went and, easy as anything, straight down our valley, tumbling down in crashing landslides on top of the carefully laid pipes in the stream from whence our water came.

That summer we had seen Mai working furiously at cutting away this rock with drilling equipment and never thought that by October there would be this open area behind and beside his house. By the time we arrived, that autumn, the place had been transformed, 'My word', we said, 'he's been working hard. Imagine shifting all that rock – wonder where it went?' We soon found out, when we discovered our water supply had stopped.

Ever since we bought Joumeyrac there have been dramatics with the water supply. This is the 'living with nature' bit. Several of our English friends, who have subsequently bought other houses in the region, had looked at our place and had discounted it completely, mainly because of the erratic water situation.

The Matazou, source of our water supply

To get a mains supply to the house was a very expensive project, as it was miles away from a connection. The local *mairie* (council) is supposed to organise this, and pay for it, but understandably, they were reluctant. The mayor and his councillors would have had to do without dinners for a year if they paid for our water supply and we certainly did not want to pay for it. So we happily carried on.

Much to our delight, the stream had never let us down. There had always been water – or at least Jehan had always managed to get it flowing down the pipe. To start with, when we first showed interest in buying the property, the vendor (Michel) installed an enormous 1500 litre water tank at the source to collect the water and piped it down to the house using heavy duty plastic hose, which he laid in the stream bed. All went well the first year. Then the winter rains came and washed the entire tank, pipes and all, downstream.

We returned the following spring to find everything everywhere and no running water, except in the Matazou. So we went to work, hacking our way through the jungle, laying 300 metres of new heavy duty piping along the banks and anchoring it firmly in a little cement *bassin,* which collected enough water constantly to make it flow down the pipe. There were several connections down the length of the pipe, so that airlocks and debris could be cleared easily. (Did I say easily? Forget that). This arrangement worked very well the second year. The reserve tank was installed next to the house and kept constantly topped up.

There was plenty of water downstairs in the *cave* for showering and flushing, but the source level being lower than the top of the house, we had no water upstairs for washing the dishes in the kitchen sink. So a small tank was installed in the bedroom above the kitchen, which we intended to fill with the help of a two-stroke water pump. Till then, water was carried upstairs in buckets as and when needed, or the dishes were brought down. Crazy, or what! To make the water flow into the upstairs tank we needed to get some pipes through the stone roof of the *cave*.

We found a promising hole in the floor upstairs and started feeding copper piping through it. Try and imagine trying to find a way through a three hundred year old stone floor, over a metre thick, with the dust of ages settled in between the cracks. We had to do this not once, but twice, as there had to be two pipes, one flowing up and the other down. The project took two whole days of jiggling, swearing and pouring liquids down holes to find a channel, but miraculously, both pipes finally went through. We can only pray that they will never corrode or need replacing. We now had water in the kitchen. This was truly civilised. We could now have kitchen taps, a drainpipe and running water. Up till then we had made do with a bucket under the sink to catch the dirty water. Needless to say, the taps had been put in before the drainpipe so the number of times the bucket overflowed, due to our delight in using the taps recklessly, was countless. When we finally finished the drainpipe, it was so new and incongruous against the lovely old walls of the house that we promptly encouraged some ivy to grow over it.

The following year saw a second big reserve tank on the hill behind the house, duly disguised with greenery. Jehan had by now found another, higher water source which flowed until June/July so both tanks could be filled easily and water would reach upper levels without needing the pump. To reach this catchment area in the stream, he had to negotiate quite a steep slope with the help of trees, but being a mountain goat he did all this quite fearlessly. Unlike yours truly who could fall off a log even if it wasn't there. So I'd stand on top of the slope saying "Be careful, be careful" and he'd get on with 'sorting out the water' – as we called it.

Sometimes, when we arrived after a long period, there would be an airlock due to water levels having dropped, or silt collected in the pipes, which would need flushing out, so the little water pump would have to be taken down too. The descent to the water source being very steep and slippery, we thought about constructing a pathway or some rough steps. As these would be too inviting for inquisitive walkers, that idea was dropped very quickly. The latest technique was to drive the car up to the edge of the road, tie a strong rope around the tow bar and use this as a sort of abseiling device. When we are in our eighties, should we ever get that far doing these crazy things, we'll think about a chair lift. Friends had often suggested a pulley system to get things from the road to the house, but that would be much too easy.

Messing about in the garden one morning, we noticed the water had stopped flowing through the main pipe from the source. We decided it must be silted up, though this would be unusual since there was a lot of water in the stream and the source should have been quite healthy. However, the descent with the pump had to be made, and I was given the easy job of watching the business end of the pipe to regulate the water flow once the silt had been flushed out by the pumping three hundred metres upstream. Not wishing to waste a drop, I lined up several buckets to catch any water – muddy or otherwise, while the unblocking ceremony took place.

After a few moments of the pump being started upstream, there was coughing and spluttering as a bit of water came out. I held the pipe carefully over a bucket and the water stopped. Then, with a huge hiccup and major regurgitation out shot an enormous snake – wider than the pipe and at least three feet long. Needless to say, I dropped everything and, as I stared in horror, out came another one – much smaller this time. The first one was very dead but the second one decided to make a break for it and headed towards the *cave*. This was a bad decision, as if it had gone in the opposite direction I would have let it go. The thought of a small snake, which would eventually grow, living in the *cave,* was not a happy one, so without much ado, I stamped on it with my working boots, feeling cowardly and like a great big bully. Here was this dainty little creature who meant no harm and probably had no venom either, being trampled by a rather well built woman without so much as a 'by your leave'. It put up a valiant fight and wriggled bravely but victory was mine. Apologising profusely I flicked it into the bushes with a stick. The other one lay floating in the bucket for Jehan to dispose of.

The water continued to flow beautifully after that and we made sure the filter, in the form of an old sock, on the other end of the pipe, was securely in place again.

The water situation is still pretty much the same, except that now we have big rocks (courtesy of our nearest neighbour) firmly wedging the pipes in place. Mercifully, the water still flows through in spite of the rocks. In fact it has worked to our advantage as the water collects at the correct spot quicker than it did before. So all is forgiven; so far, so good. Twelve years on and Michel suggested that he could position a 3000 litre concrete tank on the hill above the house. He made it sound very easy – he used his tractor like his right hand, and if he said he could do it, it was good enough for us. We think he still feels that this little house belongs to him – he had started doing it up for his daughter who preferred the city life – as most bright French youngsters do.

Every time we undertook a new project, he would cast his eye over it for approval, or otherwise, and if it didn't come up to his expectations, he would wag his finger disapprovingly with a smile on his face saying "It will not work unless you change it to the way I suggest." (A bit like Jeeves). We had always asked his advice and involved him with everything and he probably felt responsible for any problems we might come up with. This was fine, because he kept an eye on the house in our absence. There was the time when we turned up unexpectedly in February to find our garden steps in disarray, with steaming piles of horse manure and hoof prints everywhere. He had generously given permission to his friend to graze his two horses on our land – never mind our carefully planted roses. (Well, if we were silly enough to try and make an English garden in wild French countryside, it served us right).

2003 was one of the driest summers on record in France, as well as in England. The Aveyron had not seen rain since the 15th. of February. It was also the year that we decided to place three 1000 litre tanks in the hillside behind the house to fill with water after the spring rains, so that we could enjoy the hot dry summers without worry. In January, Michel dug a deep trench with his tractor and two large plastic tanks were lowered into place. Naturally, the trench was much too narrow, so much swearing and digging by hand had to take place before they were properly installed. The big plan was to come down in June when the stream is usually in full flow and fill the tanks, after Jehan had done all the connecting pipe work, and then move the third tank from its position lower down to its new place alongside the others.

We duly came down in June, to find the Matazou bone dry – not even a damp patch. The little source of water upstream had dwindled to a drip not enough to fill a teacup, let alone 3000 litre tanks. This was a new experience for us and also, a sobering one. As ever, we looked on the bright side – this would be a different sort of holiday at Joumeyrac. We would simply have to find fun things to do other than working on house projects. First of all, we walked the length of the Matazou – a solid rock river bed worn smooth over thousands of years. It was beautiful, and in tiny pools of water here and there we found *Ecrevisses* (Crayfish) now struggling to survive but still alive. Apparently, they only live in clean water but I wouldn't take that as a sign that we could drink this stuff. We clambered down into the ravine and discovered the ruins of an old building. Perhaps it had been a water mill at one time bordering the river. There were several tracks made by the deer who came down to drink, and we also found a little natural spring further down which was still flowing, which pleased us no end. Not that we had any intention of harnessing that water at this time, but it was comforting to know that it was there. We managed to spend ten lazy days using what we had in the old tanks and collecting water from the source at Roquetaillade or in the town whenever we could.

Our French friends reacted to our shortage of water with 'when you have wine, who needs water?' drinking taking priority over bathing. Our English friends reacted with more practical suggestions, offering the use of their bathrooms any time we wished. However, we managed to stay relatively clean and sweet smelling in spite of the drought. It does make you appreciate what you often take for granted. England also had an exceptionally dry summer that year and there was a real dread of forest fires all over Europe. The landscape reminded me so much of India during the dry season – black outcrops of rock among parched yellow grass and cracked earth. Our school playground was like that for most of the year. The drought seemed to have had an effect on the slug population too – we didn't see any of our slimy brown friends – so there were some perks.

The same year, we came down for three weeks in September. It had finally rained on the last weekend in August. It must have been quite a deluge, and to our joy, the Matazou was flowing healthily when we arrived. The house was immaculately clean – no mice in the traps and all neat and tidy. Michel later explained that the mouse population had also perished because of the lack of water. The earth had dried to a depth of a metre, and all the burrowing animals had suffered. Well, we can do without mice but what about our little *Loirs?* Happily, we saw them in the *cave* - much smaller than usual, but then, there were smaller walnuts on the trees for them to eat.

The weather that autumn was spectacular – truly perfect. We swung into action and filled the new tanks, heaving the third one into place and plumbing it all in. Why hadn't we done this years ago? As the tanks had to be covered and protected from the frost, early one morning Michel appeared with some enormous old beams of wood, explaining that they had to go alongside the tanks. He also produced some old metal sheets to go across the top, all of which had to be covered with soil and weighted down with large stones so that the wind would not whip them off. He described his Master plan to us like Michelangelo designing the Sistine ceiling, and after his double *pastis*, went home, leaving us to manoeuvre the beams, fix the sheets, rake the soil, heave the stones and put in the finishing touches. We did a magnificent job – so much so, that we now have a new garden area around the tanks where we have planted lavender, rosemary and santolina accompanied by handfuls of poppy seeds scattered by my friend Barbara that she had brought from her lovely garden in Claygate.

Chapter 18: Visitors from Leafy Surrey

This was Barbara and Charles' first (and probably last) visit to Joumeyrac. The experience will stay with them forever. They were visiting a cousin, who had bought a fabulous villa near Narbonne. This was to be his permanent residence and was a converted farmhouse, with five huge bedrooms – each with an en-suite bathroom, colour coordinated down to the soap. We went to Narbonne to fetch them and stayed overnight.

It was a magnificent establishment, with an enormous garden surrounding the swimming pool, which was edged with pretty blue mosaic tiles. No modern convenience had been overlooked. Even the underwater lights in the pool came on automatically, as did the sprinklers on the lawn. Electric gates, satellite TV, the lot. This was the French house Barbara and Charles were visiting when we arrived to pick them up and take them to Joumeyrac. As they had heard so much about our little cottage with the red roof, we thought it was about time they saw it, in the raw, as it were. There was great excitement at meeting each other in France and we drove back to Roquetaillade, chattering all the way. At last, we arrived at the top of our drive and I said "Here's the drive" and they said "Where?" and Jehan went nose down the steep descent to the bridge. After a weak "Oh my goodness" from the pair of them, there was stunned silence as he drove over the bridge with less than an inch to spare on either side.

"Here we are!" Comment no. 1: "Oh my word, it's Hansel and Gretel's gingerbread cottage in the woods!" followed by, "It's Little Red Riding Hood's cottage!" and then, chuckles and amusement all round.

We showed them the bathroom in the *cave*. "Where's the bath?" "Good grief, is that the shower?" "What an amazing doorway" and more chuckles and gleeful remarks. We went up the stone steps, trying to remind them that we had constructed them with our own fair hands and laid all the flat stones scoured from the countryside to make the patio – I don't think any of this sank in – the shock of arriving here, after their sojourn in the luxurious villa was too much. Finally, Charles said 'I hate using the word, but I'm gobsmacked,' and Barbara asked us what made us do it in the first place. We explained gently that we really, actually loved it and that our boys had learned a great deal about self reliance and making something out of nothing, and how lucky we were to have found such a place.

As I spoke, I realised that they adored the house and the surrounding land, as Barbara was off taking photographs and Charles had climbed to the top of the hill to admire the view. Given half a chance, Barbara would have organised an archaeological dig to investigate the

Roman presence that was undoubtedly here. They are rather special friends who lead a relatively organised life and I feel we simply proved what they had suspected all along – we were quite crazy. We took them back to Narbonne that evening and stayed overnight in very civilised surroundings. Our bedroom had a bathroom in the shape of a horsebox – all wooden with a stable door.... and they think *we're* crazy?

The next morning, after a leisurely breakfast we tootled back home via St. Saturnin, to visit the *vignerons* and stock up on wine, after a great deal of tasting of course. We stopped for lunch at the only restaurant in St.Saturnin – not to be recommended if you are in a hurry, as the lazy hazy atmosphere of the Languedoc induces an unhurried stupor upon its inhabitants, (or is it the mist of the wine hanging in the air). Refreshed and recharged, we meandered home via country roads, laden with several cases of their choicest *vin*.

One year we decided to come at the end of October, for a couple of weeks. Friends had told us it was always beautiful, warm, sunny and autumnal. We arrived on a Thursday afternoon in the pouring rain, stopped at the top of the drive and thought about all the things that had to be unloaded from the car. As we didn't intend going out again that evening, Jehan decided to reverse the car down the drive and park it by the bridge. The drive was fairly clear of weeds, as we had been here that summer, so this seemed to be a good idea. At that time, the car in question was a large Peugeot 505 estate with rear wheel drive. Well, he reversed it expertly down while Jamsheed and I held our breath. I really do think that holding one's breath, shutting one's eyes and crossing one's fingers at times like these helps the driver immensely. I would not advise this procedure for the driver himself, you understand, however dangerous the task.

This successfully accomplished, with one or two ominously slippery moments, all the essentials were unloaded in the steady drizzle and we clumped up to the house, promising Jamsheed that it would be a beautiful day tomorrow. On the front door was a soggy hand written note from Bob inviting us to dinner that very evening, as he had two friends he would like us to meet. They were leaving for England the next morning, hence the urgency. Looking at each other, the big question was, ' Will the car go up the wet drive again tonight?' and the obvious answer in appreciation of Bob's effort in coming all the way here to leave a note was 'We can but try'. So, we settled in and cleaned up ready to go out to dinner. That last sentence sounds so simple.

'Settling in' here is quite a palaver. First you have to say 'Hello' to the house. Then you have to open all the shutters (not that there are more than two windows with shutters but they often have the odd wasp's nest inside. These are usually very small, but then, a wasp sting is quite small to look at). Next, the mouse traps have to be inspected, usually emptied or more often, thrown away, mouse and all. Then we gingerly sweep and dust and remove the plastic covers from the beds – lavender and rosemary bunches work a treat to keep little beasties away. The bed linen lives in a large metal trunk liberally scattered with aforesaid herbs. Over the years we have discovered what mice like best – they like soap. It also gives them severe diarrhoea – we discovered that too. After that particular incident (the soap in question was bright pink) we always remember to hide the soap.

Well, we sorted ourselves out, changed our clothes – nice clean pair of jeans and Jamm in a crisp white shirt – and set out. It had stopped raining by then and the sky was absolutely clear. One of those beautiful evenings when everything has been washed clean, raindrops sparkling on the autumn leaves and a few puddles glistening in the evening sun. Full of good cheer and looking forward to a jolly evening, we climbed into the car. Right. This was it. Steep uphill drive, muddy road, slippery surface, rear wheel drive, heavy car. Bad.

She went forward a few yards and at the crucial point – wheel spin. So, the lightest person got to steer, and the two heavy ones got to push. Just as well, I would rather push, anyway, than be pushed on a road like that. Jamm, fortunately, is built like a tank, and even at the tender age of fourteen was a very useful chap. The two of us pushed and pushed and, with a sudden burst of speed, the car sped away up the drive, spattering us from head to toe with sticky Joumeyrac mud. Too late to change – we were just so delighted to be on the road at last. It surprises me that both our children still loved coming here on holidays after all the torture we put them through. Still, it's all good fun, eh?

We arrived at Bob's just as he was serving dinner. They had given up on us, as with no telephone links, communication was a bit like it must have been in the old days. The couple that Bob had invited us to meet were Susan and Andrew. They had bought their house, which was not too far away from ours, a few years before us. It also had no electricity and its own source of water and they loved it. When you meet people for the first time, either something clicks or it doesn't. This time it certainly did, and we have been good friends ever since. Susan and I also share the same birthday!

They left for England the next morning, having told us what a glorious sunny week it had been for them and how lovely it was in October. Well, it rained again the next day. And the next. With a good fire going, the house was cosy and warm, but without electricity for all the naughty things like television and computer games, we were reduced to reading books, playing cards and painting. It was wonderful – even though the picture I painted was the wet view out of the front door from inside the house. Every evening it cleared up as if nothing had happened and every morning it rained. October can be like that. Mostly, a season of 'mists and mellow fruitfulness', but occasionally very wet. We gathered sweet chestnuts to roast on the fire and had our first lesson in the grand art of mushroom picking.

The French have a knack of making the simplest of tasks sound hugely romantic. Even the words *champignon, chantrelle* and *cêpes* have exotic overtones. The locations of the best mushroom forests are closely guarded secrets among the locals. So, when Therese and Max, experts in finding the best and safest mushrooms, invited us along, we were delighted. Wearing waterproof coats with hoods and stout shoes, we set off into a deep pine forest nearby with baskets and baited breath. It had rained the night before but the morning was bright and warm – perfect weather for mushrooms, apparently.

As we went further into the woods, the trees closed in overhead, blocking out the sunlight in some places. All was still and mysterious. The water dripped from the branches and the huge mounds of leaf mould and pine needles underfoot made strange shapes. It was a scene from a fairy story with toadstools and bright red spotted fly- agaric mushrooms in abundance, highly poisonous but wickedly beautiful. I'm sure the elves were around even if we didn't see them. Even the gnarled roots of the trees took on a personality of their own. Surroundings like these and a bite of a 'magic' mushroom would undoubtedly have produced a fantasy story that Lewis Carroll would have been proud of.

To start with, we could find nothing safe and edible. Then Therese showed us how to spot the best mushrooms – little white *cêpes,* hidden away between the piles of pine needles on the forest floor, which you really had to search for. We would not dream of trying this on our own – with or without a guidebook. Some of the poisonous mushrooms look almost exactly like the edible ones and some vile looking mushrooms are perfectly fine. I can't help wondering how they discovered which ones were safe and which ones would kill you. How many poor devils must have given up their lives just so we could have a good guidebook.

We returned home soaking wet with backache and a fine collection of fungi, which we eagerly cooked in butter with a touch of garlic. They were delicious. In order to appreciate any event to its fullest extent, one should not do it too often. This is as good an excuse as any not to go mushroom picking again. That and the backache and the water trickling down the back of your neck and the scrabbling about on the wet forest floor.

Autumn is a spectacular time to take a drive along the Tarn. The river flows downstream westwards out of Millau. We pick it up at the little bridge at St. Hippolyte heading for St. Rome de Tarn along the right bank. It is fairly peaceful here, then gathers a bit of momentum as it approaches the Ile de Tarn, a natural rocky island to the left of which the river flows gently and to the right, fast and furious, as the water channels itself into narrow crevasses between the boulders, splashing and tumbling everywhere. When you canoe down this stretch it is important to keep to the left of the island as capsizing in this cascade would be no fun. It is a favourite picnic spot in summer when the water levels are low but now, in autumn, it's impossible to cross over on foot.

Early morning on the river Tarn

A few hundred metres downstream the Tarn turns into a millpond – deep and green and seemingly very still. There is a strong current below but on the surface it is like glass. The reflection of the trees in their autumnal colours of orange, gold and red against the bright blue sky is fantastic. Across the river in the mountain wall behind is a troglodyte dwelling carved out of the rock – a cave house, which is used by holidaymakers.

The graceful Roman bridge approaching St. Rome de Tarn has five large arches, three of which are mirrored in the green water as perfect circles. Bright yellow-leaved trees crowd the banks, with their reflections in the still water and the whole picture is imprinted on your memory forever. If you cross the bridge, you can visit St. Rome de Tarn, which is a hive of activity in summer and absolutely dead in winter.

The bridge at St Rome de Tarn

Still following the right bank and looking across to the left bank, with St Rome perched on top of the hill, one sees a most unusual waterfall. The limestone mountainside is riddled with large holes – caves of weird shapes, from one of which spouts a heavy cascade of water, hurtling down to the river far below. There are plenty of campsites and water sports to be enjoyed here in summer and also an outdoor swimming pool, should one prefer more sanitary swimming than the beautiful river. Further on, there is a small stretch of artificial beach by the water's edge and also the 'Heron de Raspes,' a sight seeing boat that takes you down the river almost up to Pinet. The thickly wooded mountain slopes come straight down to the water – there is no mooring space or bare earth, leaving wild birds to nest freely in the rock crevasses and trees along the banks. One could imagine being in a Norwegian fjord, deep, emerald waters surrounded by majestic mountains, with the trees growing out of solid rock, somehow finding pockets of nourishment for their roots.

The road carries on high above the river. The view from above is every bit as beautiful as that from the river and as impressive. The scene changes at every bend, and gradually the descent begins to the little bridge at Pinet. Arriving at this delightful village, nestling in its own little niche at the river's edge, time stands still. Crossing over a small rivulet on the ancient little bridge barely wide enough to take a car, one could be forgiven for not realising that a few metres further on is a huge hydroelectric dam –

the Barrage of Pinet – across the Tarn. It makes ecological sense that these great rivers of France should be harnessed for hydroelectric power even though it detracts from the natural beauty; but there is still plenty left!

Leaving this enormous concrete construction behind, the road winds its way up the mountain towards Brousse le Chateau. You can go directly to Brousse but, if one is time-wasting and enjoying the scenery – when you see a bridge, you cross it to see what's on the other side. This one was sign posted for Ayssenes and Le Truel. Thinking it may be a short cut and perhaps an even prettier route, we took it. The road wound its way up to a tiny village. We drove to the very top and stopped in the village square, looking dubiously at the signpost for Le Truel pointing straight ahead. It looked a trifle narrow and sure enough, it was for walkers only. Even we weren't daft enough to go down it – so, about turn and across another pretty bridge, down to Le Truel and then on to Brousse le Chateau, which sits majestically upon its rock overlooking the Tarn.

The castle dates from the 10th century. The fortifications are in remarkably good condition, with various bits added on through the middle ages. It holds the usual dark secrets. There is the sad story of a little princess being locked up in the tower – in fact, her bed, her chair and commode are proudly on display in the circular prison. Today there is much to admire in the stone construction of the chateau with its Romanesque bridge over the moat. The old village is charming too. It is classed among the Most Beautiful Villages of France with a 15th century church and has a fine restaurant in a picturesque riverside setting.

Gazing at this wide and gentle river it is hard to remember that this is the same water that carved the Gorges du Tarn millions of years ago – still flowing without rest to join the Garonne – carrying with it all the debris of past religious wars, historic events, great and ordinary achievements of mankind with it, down to the great oceans that form three quarters of our planet.

****

A ga*ufre* is a waffle, delicious eaten with butter and honey or golden syrup. A *gouffre,* on the other hand, is a swallow-hole.

A swallow-hole is the geological term for an enormous hole in limestone rock plunging deep into the earth. An example of this natural phenomenon is the Gouffre de Padirac, south of the Dordogne, which has an underground river flowing through it. This great depression in the earth, according to local legend, had been caused by the Devil stamping his foot in anger and given that limestone is a fairly soft and breakable rock, this seemed like a plausible explanation. We never found out what caused the Devil to lose his temper, but then, he's an unreasonable chap at the best of times.

Underground river at Padirac

We arrived on a sunny summer's day with all the other tourists and their mothers to see what it was all about. The entrance to the extremely long descent of stone steps is simple enough, but as it gets darker, deeper, colder and wetter, it's easy to imagine that you are approaching the river of Hades, menacing and mysterious. Where will it take you? What lies beyond? Will the boatman from Hell be waiting to ferry you down the river? Yes, he was – big and jolly and poling a substantial punt which carried eight people into the abyss. The water was clear of all algae since it never saw the sunlight and, apart from gentle shadow lighting here and there, all was left much as it was – obviously made safer for all the visitors and children who came in large numbers throughout the season. We were taken on a boat ride in the dark, under looming overhangs of rock dripping ominously and reflecting ripples from the water. The circuit brought us back very near to the starting point but the main branch of the river flowed away underground for many kilometres, going quietly on its lonely journey through the dark, ending who knows where.

Chapter 19: Construction and Deconstruction

The house was now becoming very comfortable after the first three or four years. We had a gas-operated fridge, plenty of water, an Ascot heater for hot water showers and a rotary clothesline. (We made it a point to use only green towels, so they didn't scream at you while they were airing), and we used strictly biodegradable soaps and no bleach or chemical cleaners so as not to upset the natural balance of the *fosse*.

The gaps in the walls had been painstakingly filled with a mixture of sand, cement and plaster coloured with a brownish powder to blend in with the stones. The wall upstairs was built into the mountainside and covered with *crepi*, which is a rough type of plaster. On this wall I painted a grapevine, complete with bunches of purple grapes. Using acrylic paints seems to have been a good idea as it still looks very fresh. Why don't we paint pictures on our walls in England anymore? (Don't explain – I know. You can't take it with you when you move house).

One wall had an odd shaped hole in it. Some four or five rocks were missing. Instead of turning it into a proper window, we left it as a nature window surrounding it with a square frame and glass. Now and again some little creature comes and observes us from the outside.

Speaking of mice – we always needed to put a few traps down when we left, and that was the only disagreeable part about arriving here after a long absence. There was usually some poor creature in the traps. I say usually, because one time Jehan had put salami in the traps. None were touched except one, by a very large slug. So now we know that slugs like salami and I have never seen slugs as big as the ones we had there.

The morning after a rainstorm it was a perilous descent to the loo in the *cave*, side stepping large brown slugs with a hangover and a full bladder. (That's us, not the slugs, you understand). 'Why not build a bathroom upstairs?' you ask. There is water and plenty of space behind the house – surely that would be a good idea! In fact, why not build an extra room for your friends to visit so they don't have to share your bedroom. Well, therein lies a tale.

A couple of years after we bought the house we received a request for a *Cote d'Habitation* (a tax on residential property) and a *Taxe Foncière* (rates, to you and me). Fair enough, they were not very much so we started paying them like any good citizen. Then we went along to the *Mairie* (council office) up in Montjaux to ask if we could build a little extension on the back of the house. The mayor's secretary found all our details, the plan of the property etc. on her computer and said *"Monsieur et Madame, votre maison n'existe pas."* And sure enough, there was no house marked on the plan. Nothing. So we told her that we paid habitation tax for living in this house so it <u>must</u> exist – we wanted to build an extension to it! She looked at us patiently, shrugged her shoulders and said that we could do what we liked, as our house did not exist and therefore the extension also would not exist. Our friend Andrew was with us at the time as our French was still not up to scratch – so we said 'Thank you very much' and went home to build our non-existent extension.

On our return to England that year, we excitedly drew up plans for the extension, researching damp-proof courses and the like because, of course, we intended to build it ourselves.

Each time we came down to the house we built a little bit more, breezeblock by heavy breezeblock carried lovingly up the steps. We bought them twenty at a time from the local factory 10 km away, mixing cement, at first by hand, then borrowing Bob's cement mixer and Bob as well. We did a little work every holiday and it was coming along very well. We had plenty of help from friends and our boys worked hard too. The outer wall that would be slightly visible from the road, we intended to cover in stone. The roof was to be an extension of the existing one –

it would look just like the rest of the house. There were no neighbours to appease, no other houses in the vicinity as we were in splendid isolation.

We had completed building the walls and were ready to start construction of the roof. On Michel's recommendation, off we went to the sawmill at St. Beauzely and ordered the timber for the roof beams. This was a father and son operation that offered personal service with pride. We chose beautiful beams of solid pine, treated and cut to the proper size. They said they would deliver them to the house and Michel offered to come with them. The boys were not with us that time, so I thought, 'Great, four strong men, they can carry them down the long drive and up the other end'. Well, they arrived – three strong men. They unloaded the beams off the truck and laid them carefully at the top of the drive as, understandably, they did not think their lorry would negotiate the steep slope. Ten heavy, wooden beauties. Then followed a highly animated discussion about how two men could carry two beams together down the drive and Oh, the job would be done in no time – *'C'est facile, c'est pas lourd!'* (not heavy). At this point we were so pleased with them and so happy about everything, that Jehan gave them their money. Yup. Big mistake. They said 'Thank you very much' in their best French, shook hands heartily, climbed back into their truck and left.

There we were, with ten enormously heavy wooden beams to transport downhill and uphill and up steps for two hundred metres. Him and me. We laughed helplessly for a while at this ridiculous situation and then Jehan said 'We could tie them two at a time on the roof rack of the Cossack and drive them up'. The 'Cossack' being a four wheel drive Lada Niva – very popular amongst the farmers in France as it goes everywhere, does anything asked of it and is built like a tank. We had bought one of these amazing vehicles a couple of years earlier. In Surrey it looked like a 'yuppymobile', but in the Aveyron it was the most practical and sensible workhorse ever, as it managed to reach places most other four wheel drives couldn't. We have always had interesting cars – never anything conventional.

We lifted each beam onto the roof bars of the Cossack and tied them on securely two at a time. This was going to be a tricky operation, as the bridge over our little stream had a very tight turning circle and a steep uphill slope round the bend. In addition, it was surrounded by trees and sheer drops on both sides. It could have been the classic ladder held sideways trick if we weren't careful, as the beams were much longer than the car. We gingerly drove down the drive – OK so far – and helpfully holding our breath, up the other side and all the way up to the top behind the house. Two down, eight to go. It took us an hour and a bit, but we did it and were truly pleased with ourselves. Stacking the beams neatly, we covered them up, tied them straight so they wouldn't warp and had everything ready for our next visit when we planned to get the roof into place.

As ever, we spoke to Michel regarding the roof construction and he offered to get some supporting brackets ready for us so that we did not waste time on our next trip and could simply slot the beams into place and continue from there. Brilliant, we thought, and returned to England.

For the next couple of months we dreamed of extra space, designed a little bathroom, mentally chose tiles and even bought another wood burning stove, all ready for the new *engrandissement*. We had friends offering to come and give us a hand to put the beams up and the tiles were organised too. So nothing prepared us for the sight that greeted us on our return to Joumeyrac that summer.

The Drive.

Michel, in removing the edging tiles from the roof, had discovered a massive infestation of ants in the roof boards, so had removed more tiles and poured kerosene on the boards (luckily he's not a smoker). The ants had obviously bitten and annoyed him thoroughly, as when we arrived all was in a big mess – broken roof tiles everywhere, absolute chaos. We went over to see him for an explanation and he told us about the ants, so we said, 'Fair enough, we'll sort that out first'. Then he said, rather sheepishly, 'I think you'd better ask for planning permission before you finish this extension'. Just like that – ten years down the line. We could not understand this sudden desire to follow the letter of the law. After all, our house did not exist so our extension would not exist either. Simple logic – so, why this unreasonable suggestion at this stage?

All was made clear soon – Montjaux had a new mayor. He was younger, more energetic, leaner and meaner than the old mayor and he wanted everything brought into line – no sloppy handshake agreements and everything on paper tied up with red tape. He seemed to have terrorised everyone into good behaviour and sounded like a really strict headmaster. We decided to go and see him to clear things up. He turned out to be pleasant enough but definitely a man who went by the book. "Yes" he said, "First you must put your house on the map and then you must get planning permission. Now we have to do everything properly." When we told him we had been paying habitation taxes for ten years –

it's not as if nobody knew we were there, he said 'All the more reason for putting your house on the map' and he assured us that we would get the *permis,* so why not do it properly.

We had to visit the DDE in Millau (an extensive and mysterious organisation that deals with town planning, highways and all manner of everything), and the *Cadastre* (Planning Office) to have our house marked on our land. So we went to the DDE. We were told to sit and wait in reception, as the Monsieur upstairs we needed to see was busy. While waiting, we watched the receptionist. He was a large gentleman with moustache and glasses and he sat at his desk with a tray full of papers on either side. From one tray, he wearily took a paper, stamped it firmly with a rubber stamp and put it in the other tray. Every time the phone rang he gave an exasperated sigh and answered it, shook his head, shrugged his shoulders and carried on rubber stamping. We wondered what he would do when he ran out of papers. He did. He then began taking them from the full tray, produced a different rubber stamp and carried on till they were back in the first tray, stopping frequently to answer the phone and raise his eyes heavenwards. At one stage he looked up at us and said something to the effect of 'A French bureaucrat's work is never done' and sighed heavily. We tried to look sympathetic, and by this time we had so enjoyed the entertainment we had forgotten what we had come in for.

When we finally got to see His Nibs upstairs, he was extremely helpful and enthusiastic and advised us to draw up plans for nothing bigger than 20 sq. metres and to submit it as an *'Abris de Jardin'* i.e. a garden shed for which formal planning permission was not required, only a *'Permis de Travaux'* which was quite a simple affair. But first we must have the house marked on the map.

Next, we went to the *Cadastre* office. This was a rather interesting experience. They were quite apologetic about the fact that we had been living in this house for ten years or more, paying taxes and they had omitted to note it as a habitable dwelling. They promised someone would be along *'toute suite'* to take measurements and sort it out. The reason this house had never been marked was simple. It was originally a *'Maison de Vigne'* built some three hundred years ago and had lain as a ruin for many years. Ruins are so plentiful in this area of France that they don't bother marking them on maps, so although on our title deeds it says *'une petite maison avec terrain'*, Michel had never got around to asking the proper authorities to measure it and mark it on the proper maps, as we were expected to do this. In England one usually buys a house that is already marked on a plan, so this idea did not even cross our minds!

The following afternoon, a young couple arrived with a tape measure and a ball of string. They measured the existing house as best they could. They guessed the dimensions of the bits they couldn't quite reach and asked us if we would like them to include the proposed extension as well. We virtuously said "No, we have to get permission for that." Had they made it clear that we could have quietly gone ahead and finished the extension without a permit, as it would have already been measured as a larger house, it would have saved a lot of bother – but it would have been more than their job was worth, to actually tell us that! We were told to come and collect a copy of our new, improved plan with house the next day. We duly turned up and were presented with the plan with a little square denoting the house. I think we could have done that ourselves. At least we did not have to pay for any of this.

Armed with the new plan, we drew up all the necessary diagrams and took photos and measurements. Everything in triplicate (after all, there is a lot of rubber stamping to be done) and presented it all to the mayor, who would review it and forward it with his recommendations to the big white chiefs of the DDE at Rodez, the departmental centre of bureaucracy, miles away – how do they know what goes on in little Roquetaillade? Does anybody care? We were told we would hear from them by the end of November.

Fully expecting to get the go ahead, as the plans were for an 'Abris de Jardin' under 20 sq. mts. we returned to England quite relaxed and waited for the confirmation. The letter from Rodez finally arrived and we opened it with excitement. The permission had not yet been given because we had omitted to mark our electricity point and water supply on the application. So we sent a letter back, our French improving by the day, explaining we had no electricity or mains water as the water came from the stream. We also pointed out how isolated the cottage was and how it would not affect anyone else. It was a nice, friendly, British sort of letter.

They weren't impressed. We received a reply a month later turning down our request on the grounds that should there be a fire, the fire engines could not get down the drive and we had no fire hydrant. But what about the existing house we wondered, doesn't it warrant a fire engine if it were ablaze? – how absurd is this business going to get? To top everything off, a week later we got another missive from Rodez saying that one of their officials had been to visit the house and discovered that we had already begun construction. This was illegal and we would have to demolish it immediately, otherwise we would have to go before a tribunal in Paris. When rubber stamped documents arrive in French, complete with judicial logos and the like, *'Liberté, Fraternité & Egalité'* go out of the window. We were really shaken up. Illegal? *Nous*? Never. We had tried to do everything correctly and by the book. We had asked right at the beginning and done everything as we had been advised. Now they wanted us to demolish our hard work by the 1st of March.

I composed yet another long letter in French as my language skills were getting better by the minute. I even knew the French for 'the powers that be' and 'pompous git' though I didn't use that one. Explaining how this had been a family project over the years with the blessings of the local *mairie,* painstakingly undertaken bit by bit every holiday – how short our *vacances* were as we all worked so hard in England most of the year. It was a letter that would have melted the hardest heart. I even explained how ecologically sound the house was, not using any electricity, not polluting the atmosphere etc. It was a lovely letter telling them what respectable citizens we were, never having done anything knowingly illegal in our lives – could they not simply leave us alone to get on with our little holiday project? Well, after such a superb letter we expected a somewhat favourable reply. Well, favourable it was but not in the way we wanted. Instead of the 1st of March, they had kindly agreed that we must demolish by the 1st of August.

In the midst of the extension drama, we arrived at Roquetaillade one day to find an officious looking notice stuck to the front door. It was from the local Gendarmerie commanding us to present ourselves with our passports at the police station at 9 am the next morning. Assuming that this was all to do with the extension, we were really quite apprehensive and spent half the night worrying about being locked up in the Bastille and having our passports confiscated for ever. Jamsheed had already said he would not be coming with us to the Gendarmerie as somebody had to be available to bail us out. He would not be allowing us to take his passport either.

After a sleepless night, we dressed very respectably and went up to St. Beauzely to meet The Commandant. (the fact he was called The Commandant was fearful enough, having seen a lot of WW2 movies). We got there at two minutes to nine. The Commandant had just popped out to get the *baguette* for lunch. They obviously had their priorities right – important Police business – lunch. So we waited.

He arrived at five minutes past nine, apologetic and very friendly. We shook hands and sat down facing his desk. I clutched my handbag, which contained the passports. He never mentioned them. He asked us various questions about the house, the extension, our family, our work – everything except passports. I glanced at the blotting paper work surface on his desk and jotted in one corner under today's date was this list, which read '*Pain, les Anglais, Fromage, Vin*'. Jobs for today. Well, the first two were almost accomplished. As we finally got up to leave after this perfectly cordial and cheerful, though aimless, chat he asked us for our passport numbers – only a formality and something we should have done many years ago. He scribbled the numbers down and handed them back, shook hands, smiled, clicked his heels and amiably escorted us to our car. Presumably he then went in search of cheese and wine. We went back home in search of a large coffee in celebration.

By this time we were quite fed up with French bureaucracy, letter writing and extensions. We decided then and there to demolish what we had built so far, leaving just a metre high wall to make a nice patio for parties and, as it was purely a summer house, we'd cut our losses and reduce our stress. (Bureaucratic clout only starts above a metre high). But before we did that, one more French manuscript had to be worded – to let them know exactly what we thought of them. Yes, we would demolish but we were truly disappointed in their officialdom and whatever happened to *liberté* and *egalité* let alone *fraternité* – we almost used the French for 'pompous gits'.

So that was that. Several of our French friends including Michel said we should have fought it out but we're great believers in 'Que Sera Sera' – some things have to be put down to experience and are really not so important. Bricks and mortar are not so vital in the grand scheme of things – our peace of mind and sense of humour is what matters. We had proved to ourselves we could build a fine construction and it had been fun to do.

It had also made us very fit and strong and very knowledgeable. I now know that mixing washing up liquid into the cement mix makes it more pliable and that wetting breezeblocks before building makes them stronger and that putting metal rods into corner joints is necessary. Oh, I learned a lot of things including how to load a wheelbarrow so it didn't tip over on its side full of rocks. It was all very satisfying. Not for us the bungee jump – running downhill behind a barrow load of rocks is much more a test of skill, especially for the more delicately nurtured. It's probably something to do with the fact that I did have a very precious childhood, being born in India, the younger of two children, pampered, cosseted and never allowed to get very dirty. Well I'm certainly making up for it now.

The following May, as planned, we went down to Joumeyrac and made a rendezvous with Michel and his trusty tractor. He arrived early on a wet Wednesday morning and after the mandatory slug of pastis, drove the tractor high up on the slope behind the extension wall. He backed the tractor up to the edge of the drop behind the wall. I had visions of a somersaulted tractor and didn't want to watch. As the tractor was still some distance from the wall he had to attach a long wooden beam as a battering ram to do the job. This all looked very 'Heath Robinson' but Michel knew what he was doing. With a slight push of the tractor the walls of Jericho came tumbling down, leaving a metre high wall all round –and a very big mess. It was quite sad but it was done. We left it all as it was until the summer holidays. With some luck the Mayor saw it in its sorry state and realised (too late) how much better it would have looked if he had let us finish it in the first place, without causing such complications. Not that anyone could see any of it from the road to begin with.

It's all cleared up now and next year we are planning to put up the wooden roof beams anyway and a transparent roof to make a sheltered patio area. Later on, a wall or two, who knows...... but paper work? No way. It's not worth the effort and it's nobody else's business anyway. As I said before, a sense of humour is the most important attribute in human nature. Without it, small problems become large ones and stress gets out of proportion. The drama of the walls has improved our French no end, made us fitter, perhaps a bit wiser (but I doubt that) and the rubble from the broken breeze blocks has made a lovely firm surface on the drive where it used to get soggy in the rain. So there.

Chapter 20: French Weddings

We also did some fairly normal things on holiday at Joumeyrac, like parties and excursions to the seaside, walking through wild flower meadows and going to weddings. The first French wedding we went to was quite an experience. Our friends Genevieve and Michel sent us an invitation for the marriage of their son, Guy, to a beautiful girl from St. Beauzely. The wedding ceremony was to be held at the village church at 4 pm followed by dinner at 8 pm in the Chateau de Lugagnac near Riviere sur Tarn on the way to the gorges. Needless to say, we were quite excited at being part of such a special event and duly arrived at the Catholic church of St. Beauzely, very smartly dressed and expecting a traditional wedding. I wore a hat but the only other hat in sight was on Genevieve, the bridegroom's mother. She always looked like a fashion model no matter what she wore. Bearing in mind that the bride was a local farmer's daughter and the groom's family were practically nobility, the guest list was unusual to say the least, each dressed in his or her Sunday Best.

The variety of fashion on display was amazing, from white leather shoes with black shiny trousers (this was the men), and cotton shifts to strappy satin dresses. City chic and the local peasantry. The charming bride was one of the prettiest girls I have ever seen and along with the groom, was greeting all the guests before the wedding. There was much kissing on both cheeks (three kisses down in the Aveyron), hand shakes and back slapping. The atmosphere was wonderfully relaxed and we all sat in the church wherever we wanted. Everyone settled down noisily, in keeping with the loud recorded pop music carefully chosen to create the right ambience. Then the padre arrived, welcomed the congregation and the groom took his place with the best man to await the bride.

She arrived down the aisle with her father and the ceremony began. Much to our amusement, the entire service was sung, by the priest, in Latin. It was quite a long service and lasted about an hour, but while the rings were exchanged everyone chatted to each other. Several photographs were taken and the rings were removed and reinstated in different poses for whoever wanted to take a picture. The video camera man was practically under the bride's skirts at one stage trying for a shot of the ring exchange from below – at least we think that was his intention.

Incidentally, the best man was wearing a bright green suit and the priest posed for a few photos too – all this in the middle of the marriage service. At least the witnesses could not fail to notice that there was something going on, although it is quite possible that some of those deep in conversation with each other throughout the entertainment missed the whole event. Nobody seemed to be upset about anyone's behaviour – we were quite bemused by this refreshingly tolerant attitude to utter chaos.

After the church ceremony, there were drinks and canapés in the courtyard with wine and nibbles in abundance. The atmosphere was very friendly but after a while we wondered what we were going to do till dinner at 8 pm, which was another three hours away. We had made friends with a Belgian couple during the ceremony, who suggested visiting Compeyre, which is a pretty little village on a hill on the way to the Gorges du Tarn and quite near the Chateau de Lugagnac, where dinner would be waiting. We spent a lovely evening with them in Compeyre, which has one of the few remaining measuring systems for grain from medieval times carved out of stone in its market square. This was an ingenious and very effective way of paying the farmers on the volume of the grain rather than on weight.

The Chateau de Lugagnac was straight out of a fairy tale, complete with turrets and a little bridge over what was originally the moat; not too big and certainly not small. However, dinner was not actually inside the chateau but in a purpose built modern hall in the grounds. Long tables were set for dinner with white table cloths and pink place settings, with a large area reserved for dancing and a disco at one end. We were placed with the groom's parents and their friends at one of the long tables, while the bride and groom and their closest friends were at the high table across the top. The bride's parents sat with their friends across the room.

On reading the menu, which was printed on a scroll tied up with burgundy ribbon, we discovered that there were at least nine courses. The immediate thought was, 'We'll never get through all that!' Little did we know. The starter arrived promptly at 8 o'clock: a lovely slice of *pate de foie gras* with a small salad. It was delicious and was polished off enthusiastically in readiness for the next course. This was to be a champagne sorbet but before it arrived, one of the family members stood up and proposed a toast to the bride and groom. Then the bride's younger sister and her friend got up and read a poem they had composed for the married couple and sang a little song. We applauded and admired – it was really sweet. Then the bride's mother got up and everyone cheered wildly as she burst into song – unaccompanied and unaided by any alcohol that early in the evening. She sang lustily in a local dialect and although we didn't understand a word, we enjoyed it thoroughly. It was quite a long *chanson* however, getting on for 9 o'clock and there were eight more courses to get through.

The next day being Sunday, we had invited eleven friends to dinner at Joumeyrac, thinking we would do all the cooking on Sunday morning, as we didn't expect to be out too late the previous evening.

Well, after Mother finished singing and everyone finished applauding, there was some excitement going on at the other end of the table, and to much clamouring and cheering, Grandmother then got up to sing. She was a generously proportioned lady of some eighty years who, had she been wearing a low cut velvet gown, could have filled the curve of a concert grand piano on any operatic stage. She had a tremendous voice and sang an even longer song. We gave up on the sorbet and enjoyed the spontaneous entertainment. However, it was certainly not over when the fat lady sang.

The sorbet arrived and there was a hush while it was consumed and the third course of fish followed almost immediately. By now, it was almost eleven o-clock and we had six more courses to go. We thought maybe – just maybe, we'd make it home by midnight. Well, that's when the disco started and everyone got up to dance. So we danced. It was great fun and highly energetic and I could see sense in wearing trainers and jeans to the wedding. Why don't we do that in England, I wonder. By this stage, we were past caring about getting home at all – one couldn't really leave before finishing dinner. It would be unforgivable and the old folks were coping with it very well (they had probably had an afternoon siesta to prepare for this marathon – but nobody warned us)!

The disco, like all discos, played at maximum decibels. We danced the Lambarda, the Macarena, the Conga, the Hokey-Cokey and the French version of Knees up Mother Brown (*Levez les genoux, Maman Brune*), finally sitting down for a break at about 1.15 am when the meat course was served – I think it was roast beef. Then followed another frenzied dancing session with the help of an accordionist. This was the serious ballroom stuff – we did not dare to step onto the floor as the oldest members of the party whirled round and round, causing us to marvel at how those tiny feet could support such healthy appetites at such speed. After some forty-five minutes of excitement everyone settled down for the cheese course. Home time was getting closer. Then came the high spot of the evening.

A chair was placed upon a table, the bride in her beautiful white dress was placed upon the chair and a garter was slipped onto her exposed knee. This was an old peasant tradition at French weddings – the idea being to raise money for the newly weds to start their new life together. Once the garter was in place, all the men folk threw ten francs into a hat to raise the garter up the leg by ten centimetres and all the ladies threw more money to bring it down by ten centimetres thus preserving the girl's modesty. So it started: *'Decendez!'* shouted the women tossing their coins into the hat. *'Montez!'* shouted the men and the garter went higher and higher. Our friends, the groom's parents, did not approve of this custom but as the bride's family were in charge of the night they had to go along with it. The poor girl sportingly went along with everything. It appeared that by then everyone had lost interest in the rest of the meal – not surprisingly as the bride did have amazingly good legs.

By 3 am we were very tired and becoming a bit glazed. Several of the children were already asleep in corners of the room and several elderly guests were looking decidedly the worse for wear. I leaned over bravely to

Genevieve and said we were very tired – would it be alright if we left quietly so as not to disrupt the party? After all, being foreign, I thought we had an excuse to behave improperly and leave before the coffee (after which presumably they would cut the wedding cake by which time it would be 6 am). Much to my surprise, she looked almost grateful and said "*Mais, oui!*" and would we please give her mother a lift home – so our plan to slip away discreetly was echoed by some twenty guests who were getting quietly desperate and not wanting to be the first to mention home and bed. We gained twenty friends for life that evening; they all went "*On y va*"and got up to leave.

Earlier that evening I had enquired where the couple would be spending their honeymoon night and was told that it was a big secret, but they had booked a very expensive suite at the most exclusive hotel in Millau. Well what a waste that must have been. Apparently they reached the wedding cake at 7 am and that was followed by onion soup for breakfast. Where do these people get their energy from? Very sadly, the golden voiced grandmother died of a heart attack the very next day.

We arrived home at 4.30 am and to our amazement, found Daraius and Becky asleep in their car at the top of our drive. They had decided to surprise us on their way back from a holiday further south and finding the house locked up, waited, as they had no choice. We knocked gently on the car window to be admonished with, "Mum, Dad, what time do you call this?" Sort of thing we used to say to him. Our dinner party the next evening was very successful despite almost falling asleep in the pudding. When I mentioned we had been to a wedding the night before, our friends were amazed we were home at all as French weddings have been known to go on for three days.

The following year we were invited to another wedding in Montjaux, that of Max and Therese's eldest daughter Jeromine, (of oyster fame), to a charming young man called Erick, from Paris. Jeromine had asked me to make her wedding dress and came to London for her fitting. The next time she saw the dress was two days before the wedding when we took it down to France. How laid back is that? I knew it would fit perfectly but she wasn't to know that. It did, of course! I was invited to the house to join all the women in dressing the bride and making her up and all that sort of thing. Timings were all over the place – nobody was rushing to do anything and one of the guests was barefoot throughout the entire proceedings.

Mother and mother-in-law both wore hats and were very elegantly dressed. The Parisian bridegroom wore one of those designer outfits which look like they are two sizes too big, in crisp, white linen which creased admirably and black (no doubt very expensive) trainers. No kidding. We all walked up – half an hour later than planned - to the *Mairie* where the old mayor was waiting in full mayoral regalia to perform the civil marriage. As many of us as possible were packed into the tiny office to witness the happy event.

After the signing ceremony we all walked down to the ancient church for the service. The church was beautifully decorated by the girls themselves with corn dollies and bunches of lavender on the ends of the pews. Max had composed a special piece of music for his daughter's wedding and Jamsheed had the honour of playing it on the church organ. We were very proud of him. It was a very happy occasion.

After the service, the couple climbed right up to the belfry and everyone took spectacular photographs of them standing on the edge of the bell tower some fifty feet above, locked in a passionate embrace. Fortunately, it was not a windy day and nobody had the urge to pull on the bell ropes to send the bells pealing.

The entire village gathered in the field below, sitting on rustic wooden benches and taking in the breathtaking views across the valleys to Roquefort, enjoying more than a few glasses of wine and canapés in the balmy evening sunshine. We passed the time in idle chatter before proceeding up the hill to the village square where the wedding feast was to be held.

The *repas* this time was *al fresco,* in the square where they usually played boules. There were long tables laid out with white tablecloths and paper plates and a simple but delicious menu of ratatouille, tabbouleh and various salads. One of the local farmers had presented the family with two sheep, which were being roasted slowly on open spits since early afternoon. Being used to buying our meat already clinically carved and packaged, this was not a pretty sight but we didn't doubt that it would be delicious. We also thought we would be dazzled by the carving skills of the local butcher.

When the time came, an entire roasted sheep was paraded round the tables with much singing and clapping and then placed on a table to be carved. Along came Monsieur le Chef Extraordinaire, brandishing two huge carving knives with which he did a little jig, swirling them about in the air with a great flourish. He bowed and curtsied and made a great impression. Then he put the shiny knives down, picked up a large, earthy hacksaw and, donning a heavily blood stained butcher's apron, proceeded to saw his way through the meat. True to French style, it was under done and very, very pink – in fact, the blood was still oozing out. That was it – instant conversion to vegetarianism. He continued to chop the meat up into large, no nonsense pieces – none of the finely carved slices we had been expecting. It was piled high on to large metal trays and, with blood still dripping off the sides, brought round to the tables. Of the hundred and fifty guests there, only five or six were brave enough to risk it; this was a surprise as we thought the French liked their lamb rare. I have no idea what happened to the rest of it – perhaps it was put into the oven to be cooked properly later on.   (All the wedding guests are still alive and well).

After dinner there was a surprise cabaret. Erick the bridegroom and two of his friends gave us a fire eating display. It was the sort of dare devil activity you see on special shows on television with the warning 'Do not try this at home'. There they were – albeit at a safe distance from the audience with flaming torches, which they put into their mouths and blew out huge tongues of flame. It all looked surreal against the sombre, grey stone walls of the building opposite. It was dark by now and the main source of light was one sleepy street lamp accompanied by lots of little Chinese lanterns – naked flames in paper containers strung up from tree to tree. These were dangerous enough in themselves, considering it was a mildly breezy night and added to it was the spectacle of three young men with a large bucket of petrol nearby. Fire in every direction coming out of their mouths – it was memorable, to say the least. This again, on the honeymoon night.   Risky or what? Admittedly, they were very professional in their display, and as the nearest fire engine was twenty km. away, we were thankful there were no accidents.

We danced late into the night to music performed by the local talent – a guitarist, a drummer, a saxophonist and of course the obligatory *accordioniste* who graces all French musical *soirés*. Interestingly, no provision had been made in case it rained. Well, you say, it was the south of France and it's always hot and dry in summer. Not so. Rain had been forecast but happily it held off for the next two days for the festivities to continue.

When we passed by the following evening, they were all still wining and dining and making merry at the same tables in the square and the band was still playing. It really is true what they say about French weddings.

****

One exceedingly hot summer, many years before we bought Joumeyrac, and the boys were still quite young, we went to Cap d'Agde, on the coast. It has miles of beautiful sandy beach and lots of interesting shops. Agde was an ancient Greek settlement in pre Roman times and has grown into a chic seaside resort frequented mostly by the French, with a large marina for luxury yachts. Being slightly off the beaten track, it is usually less crowded and much nicer than the average seaside town.

When we arrived in the town centre we saw some signs saying *'Reserve Naturiste'* (remember that our French was not very good in the earlier years). We thought this might be a very educational place to take the children to as it was probably a nature reserve full of flamingos and exotic birds, and perhaps, some local wild life. We followed the signs and finally drove into a large car park in front of a gated entrance. Without a moment's hesitation we got out of the car, took our sandwiches and went to the ticket office. Tickets were 15 francs each (about £1.50) and in we went, wondering where all the animals would be.

The first sight to greet us, was a man wearing, what I thought, were very tight, skin-coloured trousers and a short jacket (it was a slightly windy day). He was pushing a supermarket trolley – my goodness, those trousers were really tight! Then we saw another man and all he was wearing was a little leather purse around his neck and jellies on his feet. We tried to ignore this spectacle until we saw lots and lots of people – all going about their daily business without so much as a pair of pants on.

It finally sank in – *'Reserve Naturiste'* meant nudist camp! The reason we'd had to buy tickets was because we were fully clothed and intended to stay that way. There were plenty of others like us, fully clothed, and going about their daily shopping, visiting the cafes and walking their dogs. There were double the number of nudists also going about their daily tasks – leaning over the frozen food cabinets to choose their favourites – gives a whole new meaning to the words ' chest freezer'.

Then all the silly jokes started - supposing you were in a restaurant and the waiter spilt hot soup on your lap, supposing you met the head master and his wife taking a walk in the nuddy. All these and many more wicked images came to mind. I do not wish to cause any offence to all you seasoned nudists out there – I'm sure it's a perfectly wonderful life, but for us old-fashioned conformists all this was highly entertaining. I must say, however, that most of the skin on display should really have been covered up in the interest of aesthetics, as a lot of it needed ironing and readjusting to fit. It must be so liberating to be able to flaunt all your cellulite in public, stretch marks and all and not worry about it. We had originally thought that this 'Nature Reserve' would be educational and fun for the children. It certainly was both of these. The youngest son never let go of my hand throughout the afternoon and once, after a particularly well endowed gentleman with a shopping basket had passed us he looked up at me and said 'Mummy, aren't these people being a little bit rude?' I explained as calmly and sensibly as possible that plenty of people did this – quite natural, really – no big deal. He seemed to understand my explanation but he never did let go of my hand.

The older one, on the contrary, could have written his own joke book by the end of the day – asking for sausages at the butcher's and buns at the baker's and the like. He was in his element and hoping to meet someone he knew. We returned to our camp site that evening happy in the knowledge that now we all knew all there was to know about the design of the human body – every shape, every detail, every wobble and much that we didn't really want to know as well.

Isn't the human race fascinating in its diversity? There are some countries in the world where you are not allowed to show so much as your toes in public and here we have the other extreme of complete freedom. There is no question of which path I would take if I had to choose – except when the temperature outside dropped!

Chapter 21: Monsieur & Madame B's English Holiday

Having travelled far and wide and gained so many different ideas, we found it incredible that our friends Michel and Ginette (of Roquetaillade fame) had never left France. In fact, they had never even been to Paris. Their world was here in the Aveyron, with Millau representing the big city and they were happy. Why not? After all, we'd travelled all over the world and landed up here! We suggested several times that they should make a trip to England where we would look after them and give them a really good holiday. Neither of them spoke a word of English but we would be there to take care of things.

The first excuse was 'Don't like flying – plane might crash', then, 'Can't come by ferry – boat might sink – drive on the left? That's crazy.' Then, in 1995, the Channel Tunnel was completed and Eurostar came into service. We said 'Train, maybe?' They waited a couple of years before Eurostar proved itself safe and then, surprise – surprise, we got a phone call one January saying "We'd like to come in March for a long weekend by train!" Perhaps they hadn't realised the tunnel went under the channel with trillions of tons of water and rock above it.

We were delighted. This would be something completely different for them – *une grande aventure* – and we were being given a chance to repay some of the kindness they had shown us in Roquetaillade. So we geared up for the visit. We went to Waterloo International station and waited at the Eurostar terminal. There they were! They were so relieved to see us that I do believe if we hadn't been there they would have turned around and gone straight back to France. They had taken the French TGV from Millau to Paris and had to change from the Gare de Lyon to the Gare du Nord. Not having ever seen Paris, Ginette suggested they take a taxi, so that they could at least see the Eiffel Tower and the Arc de Triomphe. Michel decided that a Paris cabbie was not to be trusted and would definitely fleece them, so opted for the Metro instead, with the result that Ginette was not speaking to him by the time they arrived. Can you blame her?

It was wonderful to see them. They were like two children looking at the world with new eyes. The first question Michel asked on the way from Waterloo to Claygate, as the train sped along past houses and buildings was, *'Pas des volets?'* (No shutters?) We explained that nobody had shutters in England. He grinned incredulously – *'Pas des Voleurs?'* (No thieves?) To which we replied that we certainly had plenty of those, just no shutters. When we got home he asked us if we simply left our glass windows as they were when we came to France – surely they would be broken? Fancy not having shutters. Now, we had never thought about this before.

That first evening, I made a proper French meal, with plenty of fresh bread and all the courses served in true Aveyron style. We also opened a ten litre box of wine with a tap. (Yes, I did say ten litres). We imagined this would last a few days as we hardly drank (only on holiday in France) and Ginette wasn't much of a drinker. Before bedtime, I asked Ginette what they would like for breakfast. There were croissants, chocolate, bread, milk, yogurt and fruit. She said simply ' I'll have anything – Michel will finish off the chicken from tonight's dinner.' I realised that at home he would be up at 5 am and would have done three hours work before breakfast and be absolutely ravenous by 8 am, when he would have a proper meal. So I showed them where everything was, as they had the run of the house downstairs, and went to bed.

The next morning, on hearing the front door opening at 6 am, I peeped out of the bedroom window to see Michel standing in the middle of the green, surveying the surrounding houses with great interest. He was, of course, looking at the architecture and construction but to the untrained eye, he looked like a well-seasoned house breaker sizing up the neighbourhood. Then he turned his attention to the lovely trees on the green – a big Willow, several Cherries and a Copper Beech. Luckily, our neighbours had been told about our guests so nobody rang the police.

After breakfast, we did the tourist rounds and went to London. Wrapped up in layers of warm clothing and leaning into the wind, we saw the Changing of the Guard at Buckingham Palace, walked around Leicester Square and Piccadilly and had an expensive sandwich in Oxford Street. I could see that 'City Life' was not for them – or us for that matter. I don't think they had ever seen so many people in one place at one time. We also subjected them to the experience of the London Underground in the rush hour. Frankly, I don't think they enjoyed it at all and I don't blame them. We were all much happier when we returned home to quiet Claygate.

That evening we treated them to a traditional English Pub meal, determined they should enjoy *la Cuisine Anglaise* so that we wouldn't get the constant ribbing about English food when we were out in France. For all the fuss that is made about French food – take away the butter and the cream and where are you? *'Pot au Feu'* is actually boiled beef and carrots. Only, it sounds better. If the basic ingredients are good any dish is wonderful.

So off we went to the Fox on the River in Thames Ditton, following a visit to the gardens at Hampton Court across the river. The daffodils were in full bloom but, as it was a fairly chilly evening with a brisk March wind blowing, this had to be a quick visit. We found a table, ordered our meals and sat down. When the food arrived – Beef and Ale Pie, Roast beef and Yorkshire pudding, Chicken curry and rice (I did say best of British), we picked up our knives and forks and prepared to tuck in. Except for Michel. He waited patiently and when we started eating he said, piteously, *"du pain?"* Of course, we had no bread on the table. Unthinkable. We called the waiter over and asked for some bread. The young waiter looked most worried as this was not on the Pub menu. "I'll see what I can do" he said and wandered off. Michel waited. Three long minutes later the waiter returned with a furrowed brow "Brown bread or white?" "Anything – just bread please" we said. Off he went again, returning triumphantly five minutes later with two small chunks of baguette and a pat of butter.

By this time Ginette was totally embarrassed by Michel's insistence on waiting for the bread and told him to get on with it. His face lit up when the bread arrived, but only two pieces? What about everyone else and what about more bread for him? And why the butter? When you realise that in France the bread is obligatory and unlimited at every restaurant and an integral part of every meal, this must have been one of the most unusual experiences of his life. However, they enjoyed the meal very much and were thrilled when some of our friends turned up and spoke to them in fluent French. This was a complete coincidence and we were delighted.

The language barrier must have been another big revelation for them – fancy so many people in the world not speaking French! And speaking English, for that matter. It didn't stop Michel addressing every stranger in French, though. We took them shopping to Sainsbury one day as they wanted to visit an English supermarket. He promptly set up a one way conversation with the butcher, in French, who shrugged his shoulders, looked at him and said ' Don't understand a word you're saying, mate' which was just as well as Michel had just asked him if the beef on offer was free of Mad Cow disease. (This was the time the French had banned British beef). So we averted a major international crisis by smiling sweetly and saying 'He's French'.

As they were with us for just a few days we wanted to make the most of the visit and asked them what they would like to do. One of the requests was to visit an airport and watch planes taking off. It's hard to imagine the pleasure it gave us to be the ones to introduce two grown-up people to aeroplanes for the first time. They had never seen them close up, let alone sat in one. We went to Gatwick airport, which had an observation deck on the top floor. They were fascinated. We enjoyed it too, as this was something we hadn't done since our children were little. How these heavy aeroplanes manage to take off with all those people and baggage on board and land in another country far, far away in a few hours is positively awesome. We take all this for granted – we grew up with it – but it's still amazing. After they'd had their fill of aircraft roars and fumes we got back in the car and continued on down to Brighton to see the English seaside.

Needless to say, Michel kept walking round to the wrong side of the car and no amount of explaining would make him see the logic of having a steering wheel on the right. It was so that we could drive on the left, of course. *"Pourquoi?"'* He cheered up when he saw a sign saying 'STOP' just like the ones in France. *"Ah! Français!"* he said. We didn't have the heart to tell him that STOP is an English word.

It's a bad idea visiting Brighton at the height of summer, with the other half of London doing the same thing, but in March it was diabolical. There weren't many people around, but there was a howling gale and a cloudy sky so the first port of call was a cosy pub for a warm up drink. Michel never drinks tea or coffee so when it's coffee time for most people, it's *Pastis* time for him. Having thawed out a bit, we braved the sea front, leaning into the wind to keep our balance. Soon it was time for lunch.

This was when we did the most unforgivable thing. We took two French people who loved their bread, their wine, their cheese, salad and olive oil to a Fish and Chip bar on the Brighton seafront. Well – this is what one does when one goes to the seaside in England. To my bourgeois way of thinking, a plate of hot battered

Cod, lovely and crisp, accompanied by huge potato chips and a pickled onion on a cold and miserable day, is heaven. Not so for everybody. By now, the apparent shortage of bread in England had been accepted. But how about some salad? And maybe a glass of wine? The closest we got to a salad that day was the pickled onion, which was definitely sneezed at, so we did not suggest the mushy peas. All this was to be washed down by a mug of milky coffee (in Michel's case a glass of water as he didn't like fizzy drinks, either). Ginette, bless her, enjoyed everything with the grace and charm of a well brought up lady – never complaining, always content and permanently bemused by all the unusual happenings.

I decided to redeem matters by preparing a traditional French menu that evening. While laying the table I saw Jehan opening a bottle of red wine so I said "Why don't we finish that ten litre box first – it's perfectly good?" to which he replied, "That? It's empty!" From Friday to Sunday, considering that three of us had two glasses each, this was going some. But if you don't drink tea, coffee or juice what else is there?

The next day, we went to see our friends Susan and Andrew who lived in a beautiful thatched cottage in rural Oxfordshire. The men went for a walk in the neighbouring fields and Michel inspected the soil with great interest. He decided it would be very good for potatoes. Susan had invited some French-speaking friends and had made a lovely English lunch with plenty of bread, wine and salad so all was very successful and we had a really wonderful day. Early the next morning we took them back to Waterloo and saw them off on the Eurostar.

For them, it was the holiday of a lifetime. The most telling question they asked us during their visit was 'It's so beautiful here, why do you come to France for your holidays?' which proved to us how much they had enjoyed England. For us, it was the greatest pleasure to welcome them and show them so many things that we take for granted. They really must think we are quite crazy to voluntarily live in a remote cottage without electricity or running water for our holidays. But isn't human nature like that? We always enjoy something different but always love coming home. Light switches suddenly become works of art and drinking water from the tap is a positive luxury. To this day, they speak with fondness about their trip to England. We hope we have done our bit for Anglo-French relationships.

Chapter 22: Market Day in Millau

        Daybreak at Joumeyrac was signalled, not by an alarm clock or the twittering of birds, but by a very full bladder. One snuggled down under the duvet, putting off the evil moment in the hope that by some divine intervention the urge to wee would pass. It doesn't, of course, once you think about it, so up you get. Slippers on, duck your head to avoid the roof beams and descend the stairs gingerly. Turn the huge key to unlock the heavy front door and step outside. All is immediately forgiven. The sight of the fields and mountains, with the early morning dew on every green leaf, makes you take a deep breath and feel absolutely perfect. There is a heady perfume of fresh wet grass and wild thyme and the air is crystal clear. After a few seconds you remember why you are out here in your slippers and start descending the uneven stone steps to the *cave*. Having carefully flopped your way down (avoiding the slugs) with your legs practically crossed you arrive at the *cave* door and realise you have left the keys upstairs, as it is locked at night (goodness knows why – nobody is going to find it). So up you go again and do the whole journey over. Unless of course you are a chap, in which case you don't go down the steps at all.

The sun did not come up over the mountain until about 9 am, which gave us a perfect excuse to laze about in bed most mornings. However, if it was market day or if you wanted to get to the shops, you had to be properly organised because everything in France shuts promptly at 12 noon.

Market day in Millau was an erratic affair. Some months of the year it was held on Tuesdays and Fridays and sometimes Wednesdays and Fridays and sometimes only Friday, or only Thursday. In all the years we'd been here we had not worked it out. You just went along on a likely day and hoped for the best. If there were barricades across all the roads leading to the town centre, the market was on. Parking was always at a premium on Market days so you nipped into the first available space and, equipped with a large shopping basket (one of those triangular plastic lined things which you wouldn't be seen dead with in England), you followed the crowd to the market.

The atmosphere of a French provincial market is quite unique, with its complete melange of goods on offer. The noise, the buzz of activity, the smells of exotic herbs and freshly ground coffee along with the tantalising aroma of freshly baked bread is quite heady.

Today is serious market day – everything from pink, heavy duty corsets for very large ladies (where's the point, I ask you), to home made preserves, walnut cake, wine being decanted with rubber hoses from large oak barrels into plastic jugs, bottles and containers of every description, and fifty two kinds of bread – which presumably, presents the need for the corsets. The *Boulangerie* stalls offer samples of their wares to nibble and, being hungry for breakfast, everything tastes fresh and delicious, so you end up buying *Palmiers* (may as well have ten for the price of five) and *Brioche* (only a kilo or two) umpteen variations of *Pain au Raisin* and naturally – a couple of *baguettes* which would go as hard as rocks by the next morning anyway. By the time you arrive at Place Foch, it is time for a coffee (well, it's always time for a coffee).

There are several restaurants and bars in Place Foch, all of which put tables out in the main square when there is no market and it's a lovely place to sit and watch the world go by. If one were still in college, one would wear a mini skirt and dark glasses and size up the rest of the talent, much of it racing noisily round the square on 50 cc *mobilettes*, which are considered *trés cool.*

Place Foch is the centre of activity in Millau, which itself is quite an ancient town going back to Roman times. The impressive stone fountain in the middle of the square is flanked by a couple of huge plane trees which must be at least a hundred years old, their spreading branches forming a canopy over almost the entire square. Along one side is a covered walkway, where you can still see the original medieval wooden beams supporting two storey houses with wooden shutters.

Millau museum is on the other side, with high wrought iron gates leading into a small courtyard and up a wide set of steps into what must have once been a very grand residence. The museum houses a vast array of Roman artefacts found in and around Millau, as this was a very important pottery production centre in the days of the Roman Empire. There are bones from prehistoric creatures, ancient relics of stone-age man and all things archaeological that every self-respecting museum should have.

Upstairs, there is something really special – an exhibition of the great Millavoise leather industry. This was the leather capital of Europe and much of it was destined for the *haute couture* fashion trade in Paris. Exquisite gloves and garments fashioned in fine leather and suede

– embroidered, embellished, hand sewn dainty shoes and thigh high boots from centuries past, encrusted with precious stones and pearls, which must have been commissioned by kings and queens, are all on display here. The glove making industry, though nowhere near as great as it used to be, is still going strong in Millau. The word 'Elegant' must have originated here *(Gant* being glove in French). After one is dressed, the finishing touch – *'Et les gants'* (and the gloves)! The machines used for making the gloves in the nineteenth and twentieth centuries are also on display, mostly treadle operated, and paper patterns for many famous pairs of hands and feet. This is a unique museum and well worth a visit.

We find a table, which wobbles, and sit on plastic chairs as the waiter appears and takes our order for coffee. The market is in full swing – it is summer and there are peaches, plums and greengages piled high – so we buy a plateau of peaches, juicy and sweet and full of sunshine. We sample the olives – how does one choose which ones to have? There are at least fifteen varieties and twenty-five variations – stuffed with anchovies, garlic, herbs, tomatoes – all sorts. So we buy some of each, and of course, one has to buy some plum tomatoes – why do they taste so much better in France - and garlic, ropes of it, and nuts. We love the nuts – mounds of roasted cashews, almonds and chickpeas, mixed dried fruit – must have a bit of each here too. We look sadly at the live rabbits in the cages and the plump chickens staring mournfully at the crowds and for a brief moment one thinks vegetarian.

Walking on, slices of *saucisson* are offered for tasting, which is divine, so that is that. But what shall we have for dinner tonight? Why, paella of course – it's being cooked right here. Fragrant saffron rice with chicken, peppers, mussels, unshelled prawns and lots of interesting bits, all steaming away in huge paella pans – yes, we'll have a kilo of that. Barely able to carry everything, we stagger back to the car but not before we have added four pots of red geraniums (or should one say pelargoniums) to the shopping list – must have some of these – after all, we are in France.

As we wander back to our car fully laden, we hear the sound of a big bass drum. We have to stand aside, for here comes the 'Band.' There is always a band, but the pre-requisite for being a member of this one is tone deafness. Each instrument is required to be played a semitone lower or higher than the one next to it. However, great enthusiasm and lung capacity are also required, and for the bass drummer, the largest, most luxuriant moustache and a sufficiently large abdominal surface upon which to rest the drum. The third requisite, a sense of rhythm, is not essential as long as it is beaten loud enough to compete with the rest of the instruments. They colourfully and importantly march through the crowd, scattering ladies with poodles under their arms, babies in buggies and neighbours having a hobnob, till they reach the bar on the corner where they mercifully disband and order their morning *pastis,* after which they will resume battle with their instruments with even greater abandon.

The siren from the *Mairie* wails at exactly 12 noon and the market starts packing up. We join the crowds in a mad dash to find a restaurant for lunch, as the good ones fill up very fast – the French take their food very seriously indeed. Everything stops for lunch! Heaven forbid if you had an emergency, you wouldn't get much joy until after 2 o'clock. Which reminds me; just past noon is the most dangerous time to be on French roads (this is a statistical fact) as all French drivers are frantically trying to get to the best eateries to satisfy their hunger.

Chapter 23: Rita's Cabin and Barcelona

Think of French cooking and what comes to mind? Mayonnaise, which apparently, originated in Spain. Yet, the finest mayonnaise I have ever tasted was made by one Rosario D'Souza, the afore-mentioned Goan cook who worked for my parents in India. I have no idea where he learned to make it, but his method is something I shall never forget. He was a stocky, scruffy little man with permanent stubble on his chin, a faint aroma of cheap tobacco and a strong aroma of alcohol.

In true tradition he was habitually tipsy which seemed to make his cuisine exquisite. He was the best cook for miles around and the envy of my parent's friends. To make his mayonnaise, he would sit on a little wooden stool, holding a glass bowl between his knees. Cracking an egg (one-handed of course) he added a pinch of mustard, a pinch of sugar and some salt and proceeded to beat it, not with a beater or a fork but - with his fingers. With the other hand he poured the salad oil in a fine trickle, beating all the time with his right hand. It blended and thickened beautifully – then he added a little vinegar, still beating with his hand. It was fascinating to watch. The whole process must have taken at least ten minutes and the resulting mayonnaise was the most delicious I have ever had. I thought of this one day in Therese's kitchen, watching her make mayonnaise using a fork with a clove of garlic stuck in the prongs. She said that beating mayonnaise by hand was the original French way in the days of Louis V, (not sure where one stuck the garlic).

Rosario's daughter Rita, who went to work for my sister in Italy, has inherited his culinary skills. She married an Italian farmer and lives on the mountain slopes of Lake Como with several cows, making cheese, butter and all manner of rural fare, including salami from their own pigs. She also owns a little log cabin high up the mountain (one thousand metres above the lake) where she runs a little restaurant for intrepid walkers during the summer months.

Access to the cabin many years ago used to be only on foot – we attempted it once, my brother-in-law Andrea having said 'Oh, it's just a short walk up the mountain'. I nearly died in the attempt, slipping and sliding all the way as most of the walk was above the snow line and I was wearing ordinary trainers. The rest of them had proper walking boots. Having reached the top two hours later, Rita gave us huge platefuls of steaming Polenta cooked on a wood fire – a rib sticking Italian maize flour concoction laden with three kinds of Italian cheese and lots of butter. It really was a 'too far to go to eat too much' sort of day and the descent was even scarier, though much quicker. In recent years there has been so much development on the same mountain that they now have vehicular access to the top. It is tarmacked half way and then a perilous dirt track with a steep drop into the forest on one side and mountain wall on the other with hairpin bends at 45 degree angles – it is almost easier to walk and infinitely safer. Rita and her family negotiate this road every day in summer.

Needless to say, it is now very chic to own a country cabin up there, complete with picture window for stunning views of the lake far below. Rita showed us where they made their cheese, in a little room under the main building, with a concrete floor. A low wall formed a shallow bath. She assured us that at cheese-making time this room was scrubbed absolutely clean. (Today it had straw and chicken feathers here and there, not to mention other signs of poultry). Several litres of milk are poured into the bath with the culture for the cheese-making process and left to ferment. As usual, the powers that be – European bureaucratic law, says that this method of cheese production is not permitted any more. Many things have to be changed involving a lot of expense and form filling, so many of these small industries will eventually die out, but I would imagine that a few will continue regardless of the law makers of Brussels.

I must make mention here of the dog, Brandy. It was a huge Bergamo sheep dog, dark brown and very shaggy. Half way down his back his coat was like a Rastafarian hair-do, thick, curly and matted – a bit like walking around with a carpet on your back. His eyes were permanently hidden behind a curtain of hair and I cannot imagine how you start to groom a dog like this. 'Dry clean only' comes to mind. He was in his element, of course, high up in these mountains where it is always cold and, in spite of the burden he carried, he had a lovely temperament.

****

One January, we made a little excursion into Spain as it was too cold and cloudy at Joumeyrac and the weather in Barcelona sounded infinitely better. As we crossed the border we noticed the difference. The road surface became a bit rougher, the style of driving became even rougher, and the roadside café we stopped at was rougher still. With a basic knowledge of French and Italian, we thought Spanish would be a doddle. Not so, because here they spoke Catalan, The only word we could understand on the lunch menu was 'Pollo' which we translated as chicken. So we ordered that and a salad. What arrived was enough for six healthy appetites.

As we got up to leave, we heard dance music and as it sounded like a live band, we walked round to the back of the building to investigate. Steps led down to a basement and there was indeed, a live band and couples dancing ballroom style – two o'clock in the afternoon on a working day in a roadside café in rural Spain. Excellent. The wine was flowing and the place was full of truck drivers. This we deduced because the car park was packed with articulated lorries, all of which would later be driven by high-spirited routiers finishing their deliveries overnight – or manana – or whenever. The dancing and relaxing was the important thing. And why not?

We carried on to Figueras, the home of the Salvador Dali museum. There is no point in attempting a description here. It was mind blowing and well worth a visit. There is some incredibly clever art and plenty more, which will make your hair, and everything else, stand on end. Dali was definitely everything a psychiatrist would dream of – a job for life unravelling the thoughts behind his work. To each his own; what a boring world it would be if we all liked the same things. There would be nothing different to dislike.

The coastal road to Barcelona is spectacular with sheer drops down to a very blue sea, the soil being red and rich and vegetation the brightest green. Needless to say, there are plenty of holiday villages springing up in every available pocket. Wherever there is access to a bit of sandy beach, a developer has taken it over and built several holiday chalets. Happily, some areas will always be inaccessible, so one can enjoy both aspects. January, incidentally, is not the time to visit this Spanish coastline in the hope of finding somewhere to spend the night. Everything is shut. Well and truly. It does make sense, of course, nobody except a couple of die-hard British tourists would want a B&B in deepest winter on the Costa Brava, so we ended up in a Campanile Hotel off the motorway for the night.

Barcelona was fabulous. January it was, but it was warm and sunny, so we did the tourist thing and took an open top double-decker bus tour. The most exciting vistas of the city are to be seen from over ten feet above the ground. Down the centre of the main boulevard are rows of palm trees and orange trees, and among the palms there are bright green parrots, going about their daily tasks as if they were in some tropical paradise. On either side of the wide street are the most intriguing buildings. The architecture is fascinating everywhere you look. Gaudi had great influence here and also the aforementioned Mr Dali. Art is everywhere – unexpected decorations on buildings, a huge stone fish coming out of one apartment block; intricate wrought iron designer balconies. The buildings themselves are curved and quite unique. It really is rather special.

The icing on the cake is the Gaudi Cathedral (Sagrada Familia) which is, undoubtedly, the ugliest and most bizarre building I have ever seen. The Millennium Dome in London does not even come close. This thing has personality – it is compulsive viewing for its ability to annoy. It must have caused such an uproar when it was given planning permission for construction (if, indeed, it was). One guidebook describes Gaudi's use of 'Complex symbolism' providing a 'Visual explanation of the mysteries of faith!' Here we have gargoyles and lofty spires topped with what look like dessert dishes piled high with scoops of ice cream. Obviously, a good salesman who, like the tailor in the story of The Emperor's New Clothes, convinced the planning officers that only people with a true artistic eye could appreciate the exquisite design and technical skill required to construct such a monument. They must have all nodded and agreed in sophisticated assent. Either that, or somebody had a lot of money. Anyway it's there, it's exceedingly high and ghoulishly memorable.

Also, Barcelona would be no fun without it.

Chapter 24: Le Viaduc et Le Pont du Gard

Le Viaduc de Millau

Most people will agree that French roads are among the best in the world. This is partly because they have plenty of space and whenever they need a new road, they go ahead and make one. Each time we drive down to the Aveyron we arrive a few minutes earlier because a new stretch of Autoroute has been opened – straighter, faster and smoother. This is all very well, but vast tracts of countryside are being carved up. The smaller towns along the way are being bypassed (which is better for the physical health of the town but not the commerce) and faceless hotels with expressive names like 'Quick Sleep' and 'Mister Bed' are springing up everywhere. When we complain about our crowded motorways in Britain – which we do not yet pay to use – we should remember that if any widening or straightening is to be done, a hundred small farms, villages and umpteen trees with preservation orders on them will be in the way, making improvements impossible. But is that such a bad thing?

The much publicised *Viaduc de Millau* opened in 2005. Designed by one of this century's most visionary architects, Sir Norman Foster, it forms part of the A75 Autoroute. This is a grand viaduct spanning 2.4 km across the valley of the Tarn on its way to Montpellier. The most spectacular aspect of this imposing masterpiece is its height: the supporting pylons reach some 340 metres in places, the central one being 35 metres higher than the Eiffel Tower.

We had been observing the development of the bridge over the past few years with some trepidation, as it represented yet more urbanisation. Beautiful and elegant it certainly is and to give the French construction workers their due, it was completed ahead of schedule. The townsfolk in Millau had mixed feelings about it. On the one hand, they were justifiably filled with pride at having the world's newest and tallest bridge that looked so impressive yet delicate and graceful, but on the other, afraid nobody would visit them any more as all the traffic would bypass the town and their commerce would suffer. There was much discussion and argument in the bars and cafes in and around Millau about Le Pont, but it has arrived, and by the look of it, is here to stay.

To drive over it is a most pleasurable experience and it is a magnificent feat of engineering and design. Not only is it very long and very high, but it is also curved and on a slight slope. As you approach, it looks like a convoy of tall ships in full sail and if it's a cloudy day, they could be transporting you into the ether.

Le Pont du Gard   (2000 years and still standing)

Two thousand years before construction on the Pont de Millau began, the Romans built the architecturally sublime Pont du Gard. This beautiful, rose coloured structure is part of a 50 km aqueduct, which carried fresh water from the Languedoc to the Provencal city of Nimes. It spans the river Gard, which is wide and shallow, flowing quietly in its deep valley. This is truly a grand *chef-d'oeuvre,* with its three tiers of graceful arches, each tier narrower than the one below it, culminating in the water channel at the very top. This has the slightest of slopes needed for the water to flow freely and carried some 44 million gallons of water daily. History has it that the aqueduct was in use for one thousand years, five hundred of which were without maintenance. To think that this was all accomplished without electricity, JCBs or computerisation; simply mechanical manpower and architects with a vision for the future.

At present, the Pont du Gard is carefully preserved as a national monument and, although in the past one was allowed to walk upon it freely, access is only to the lower (and safer) level now. Several years ago, when we visited it with the boys, you could walk over the top, at a height of some 50 metres – an extremely foolhardy exercise as there were no barriers on either side.

Daraius on top of the Pont du Gard How did we let him do that?

The *pavoirs* beneath your feet spanned two metres but were badly damaged in places so you balanced precariously on the width of a metre along the top of the wall. There was just about enough space for two people to pass each other. In addition, many stones were missing and it was easy to lose your footing. I cannot believe that we actually walked across, and what is more, allowed our children to do so as well. A gust of wind or a fit of coughing and this book would never have been written. There were several fearless fools walking across it – some preferring to walk within the walls, which held the original water channel. This was infinitely safer, but a lot less fun. The Pont du Gard still stands, a solid and graceful legacy to the grandeur that was Rome. Will the Viaduc de Millau still stand graceful and firm two thousand years hence? I wonder.

Top of the Pont du Gard

During the middle ages travel from Millau to Montpellier was on foot and horseback, the journey often taking several days. On the way travellers would stop at La Couvertoirade, a fortified hostelry founded by the Knights Templar to protect pilgrims and wayfarers from disbelievers and bandits respectively. Stout ramparts added in the fifteenth century provided a safe refuge and shelter from the wide, open wilderness of the Larzac. Today it is a very pretty place to visit, its old stone ramparts adorned with bright baskets of flowers, charming craft shops and lovely restaurants. It is what one might call a modern, medieval village, if such a description is possible. Throughout summer there are medieval activities with jousting, music and feasting.

After Le Caylar the landscape changes over the Causse du Larzac – windswept and wild. This is a barren, lunar landscape until you reach the edge of the plateau dropping down to the Pas d'Escalette, so called because in days past one climbed down wooden ladders over the cliff edge, to the lower coastal plains. This was accomplished wearing heavy clothing and carrying luggage in all kinds of weather. There is now a sleek tunnel under the pass which one zooms through, unaware of the hardships of travel in the old days. It does make you admire the people who did travel and develop roads for our future use, finding interesting geographical features along the way. Even now, with every excavation for a new road comes an archaeological find, from dinosaur bones to ancient caves.

A few kilometres west of the Pas d'Escalette, an exceptionally tortuous mountain road takes you up to the *Cirque de l'abeille.* We drove all the way up without meeting another vehicle coming down, which was truly fortuitous. If one wanted to disappear from humanity this would be a good place. It would not be so good if your car broke down or rolled off down the valley, for you could turn into an archaeological find yourself many years from now! There is the *Grotte de l'abeille* to be visited at the very top – so named because the stalagmite formations inside look like giant bees, complete with bulging eyes. The rock is so rich in varied mineral deposits that the colours are quite remarkable. There is a little shop at the *Grotte de l'abeille* which is, amazingly, open every day of the year, perhaps in the hope that somebody will find it and having found it will actually want to buy something. If it were out of stock you could hardly ask your customers to come back the next day. Driving up here was madness enough but we passed a couple of cyclists labouring uphill as if performing some religious act of penitence. Their reward would not even be the heavenly joy of freewheeling down the other side as once they reach the top they are on the flat plateau of the Larzac.

This bleak landscape of the Larzac is home to the ancient herds of sheep whose milk is used for making the famous Roquefort cheese. The village of Roquefort-sur-Soulzon, to give it its proper title, has not risen to fame because of its beauty or quaintness. No, that achievement was thanks to a simple young shepherd who, while tending his flock of ewes one scorching afternoon, decided to have his lunch of bread and curds in the cool dark shade of a cave under the mountain.

There was nothing for him to look at, except outcrops of rock and the *garrigue*. Even his sheep looked identical to each other and very boring. So, when suddenly he saw a young woman walking along in the distance, who can blame him for abandoning his curds and rushing off in pursuit of some crumpet instead? His interest in the lass was clearly rewarded, as he did not return to the cave for a few weeks, by which time the bread and curds had turned into a mouldy, creamy mess with green streaks. He was, poor chap, desperately hungry so he ate it anyway. It was, to his astonishment, most delicious – and that was the humble beginning of the great Roquefort cheese. This story has its roots in pre-Roman times so it was very long ago indeed and should be taken with great handfuls of salt, preferably from Narbonne, as that is what goes into the cheese.

The Cambalou caves, where the cheese is matured, stretch to around two kilometres. They lie on the north side of the cliffs and are always in shadow. They are connected by narrow passages and fissures, through which cool, moist air flows, giving a constant temperature of 6 to 10 degrees centigrade and a high humidity. This encourages the spores of a mould peculiar to this environment – 'Penicillium Glaucum roquefortii' – which is the secret ingredient in the production of the cheese, (though I suspect it's the same green stuff you get on mouldy bread). Today, these spores are introduced into the curds before they are pressed into the *fourmes*, which are then brushed with lashings of sea salt from Narbonne and laid on racks to mature for four to six months and turned regularly to encourage the mould to spread evenly.

The Roquefort cheese industry now employs several hundred local people and distributors world wide – and all because a young man sacrificed his crust for a bit of lust.

One of the cheese caves underground

Regional recipes evolve according to what ingredients are available in abundance. Roquefort cheese features prominently on the Aveyronaise menu. There is Roquefort salad, crêpes au Roquefort, delectable *millefeuille* pastries au Roquefort and steak with sauce au Roquefort – which is decadently delicious. This cheese is much saltier than most other blues and my preference is for a good Stilton or even a creamy Gorgonzola but hey – who's complaining?

Early one Sunday morning we set off for a day's canoeing in the Gorges du Tarn. The most direct road to Millau from Roquetaillade follows the river, and is not very wide. It is usually quiet so one is tempted to admire the scenery while driving along. So you have a wall on your right to keep you out of the river and mountain rock on the left.

It was a peaceful morning around 10 o'clock. We were tootling along happily in our trusty big blue VW camper van when, coming towards us at great speed, headlights and Cibie driving lights flashing, was a rally car – red and bright and very fast. We slammed on the brakes and pulled as far over to the right as possible and he passed us, missing by two inches. 'Oh my goodness' we said, or words to that effect, straightened up and went on our way muttering 'Mad French drivers.' Ten seconds later, another one – dazzling white this time, lights flashing, advertising slogans plastered all over it and we thought 'Wow! We'll get to see all these rally cars. How lucky can you get?' Of course, there was nowhere to pull over on this road – at least 5 kms till you got to a decent lay-by. So there was nothing for it but to carry on, feigning blissful ignorance that we were on a National Rally route, in the opposite direction at the worst possible time. But was there anything to inform us of this event? Were there any posters, any obvious road closures or diversion signs? Any gendarmes? No. This was much too early on a Sunday morning. Only a few *Anglais* would be about and they didn't matter. Well, let's face it, we enjoyed every minute. Several drivers probably lost precious seconds, while their brains accepted the vision of a blue camper van on their racetrack with no steering wheel immediately visible (not in the right place anyway). Imagine the navigator's instructions ' left a bit, right a bit, straight on – *merde!'*

I expect many lives were in danger that morning, but hell, it was fun. And it's something to write about.

Our trusty and most versatile big blue VW Camper Van

This is not to say that the Traffic Police are not active in France. They are extremely efficient. One day, driving along a lovely country road with no other cars in sight we were stopped by a very large Gendarme, who seemed to have stepped out of the bushes. He planted himself squarely in the middle of the road and imperiously flagged us down. Hearts beating and feeling guilty but wondering what we were guilty of, we stopped. He then ponderously turned his back on us and waved a large tractor across the road from the neighbouring field. That was it. He then courteously waved us on our way with a charming smile.

Another time on our way back to England along a quiet country road, we were stopped by a group of trainee gendarmes. 'Licence? Passport?' Could we step out and let their sniffer dog check out the car? So we did. The car was full of bags of dirty linen, several cases of wine, *naturellement*, coffee, and a couple of *saucissons*. No drugs, no tobacco, no firearms, dead bodies or anything of great interest to the dog, except perhaps the sausages. Ah – the dog. He was a delightful black Labrador, wagging his tail and as cheerful as anything. All he wanted to do (and he did) was lift his leg on our back wheel. That appeared to be enough excitement for him. The gendarmes cautioned us not to touch him as he was 'a very fierce dog' (so why was he licking my hand)? They commanded him to *'Cherche! Cherche!'* and bodily heaved the reluctant animal into the car. Well he found the *saucisson,* but as he had just been fed, even that proved unworthy of his efforts. After much frustration on the part of the gendarmes and much amusement on our part, they thanked us and explained that this was a trainee dog that they were putting through his paces. I would imagine the dog failed his A levels spectacularly. We continued on our way with a warm feeling of being good citizens and having great rapport with fierce police dogs.

However, not all our encounters with the traffic police have been amusing. There was a time, before we bought the house, when we were in a hired car from Montpellier airport. Jehan was driving and, understandably, having got his hands on a brand new Renault 5, he was speeding - just a bit. Well, we got pulled over. So we quickly decided to be completely non-French speaking and very, very stupid. After inspecting the licence and passports etc. the gendarme said ' *Neuf cents francs*' which was the spot fine for speeding. This translated into ninety pounds. We pretended we hadn't understood, although our faces suddenly draining of all colour probably gave the game away. Jehan smiled and proffered a hundred franc note, shrugging his shoulders magnanimously. The gendarme took the note, jabbed it with his finger and said *'Neuf comme ca'*, and held up nine fingers. Well - we had to admit defeat. We had tried. So Jehan took out an Eurocheque and filled it out, explaining that we didn't have a lot of cash. Now this was a clever move as Eurocheques in those days were a fairly new event. The gendarme reluctantly accepted the cheque but as it was nearing lunchtime, or there was too much paper work involved, it never got cashed and we got away with a slap on the wrist. Speeding is definitely a no-no. The phrase *'Neuf comme ca'* is now a family joke.

Chapter 25: Tatjana's First Visit to Joumeyrac

When we first saw Joumeyrac, our eldest son Daraius was thirteen years old. He is now many years older, married and a father himself. His wife, Becky, is the daughter we never had and she fits into our family as if she had always been there and we love her dearly. Being a midwife by profession she has those practical, no-nonsense nurse qualities combined with affection and a great sense of humour. And she doesn't mind spiders or the sight of blood. Needless to say, she loved Joumeyrac too.

Having spent a couple of holidays here they decided, very bravely, to come down with their lovely little daughter Tatjana, then seven months old. We were already there, making the house as comfortable as possible and thoroughly excited at the prospect of our grand-daughter's first visit. Jehan screwed a large bracket into one of the beams to take her baby bouncer, I bought a new white rug and everything was cleaned and polished – well, as much as it could be. The day they arrived, in the middle of August, the temperature started rising – it was 30 degrees in the shade.

Having driven all night they reached us at 11 a.m. and Daraius was, understandably, very tired. After protests of 'I'm too excited to sleep – I'm fine,' he put his head down on the pillow and was out cold. Jehan, not having slept all night for fretting about whether they were safe, also zonked out, which left Becky and me and one very hot baby. So the three of us found the coolest spot in the house, which was the *cave*. Now, the *cave* is like the best quality air-conditioning on a very hot day – it's bliss. We took cushions and a couple of garden chairs, some drinks and snacks, put Tatjana in a basin of water to cool her down and set up camp for the afternoon next to the toilet, in the dark *cave* surrounded by garden tools, hose pipes and a cement mixer amongst other things.

After a while, Tatjana fell asleep in Becky's lap. We had just settled down to a nice, quiet afternoon when we heard a car pull up at the top of the drive. Half past two on a blazing August afternoon is definitely not the time to go visiting – so I went to investigate.

Earlier that week, Jehan and I had gone down to Cap d'Agde to visit Michel's wife, Ginette, who was staying at her little studio flat by the seaside. We had mentioned Tatjana's impending visit, and she had decided to come and see her. Well, she thought she'd be nice and visit her husband the same afternoon in Roquetaillade – surely he would be sitting at home twiddling his thumbs, so there was no need to phone him in advance. Well, Michel had decided to go into Millau for the day to watch the World Boules Tournament. So, he had locked his front door with an extra security padlock and disappeared. Madame arrived at 2.30 expecting him to be there and found herself all dressed up and nowhere to go. So she arrived at Joumeyrac to see us instead.

She looked lovely – tight cropped jeans, high stiletto heels and lots of makeup, with her little *toutou* Roxy tucked under her arm and carrying a designer paper bag with a designer dress in it for our granddaughter. She apologised profusely for the untimely arrival, as did her daughter Christine, who had also come up specially. They tripped delicately down the drive as I went up to greet them, welcoming them with hugs and kisses. They followed me into the *cave*, with me behaving as if this was the most normal place to entertain one's guests. *"Asseyez-vous!"* I insisted, opening up another folding chair and shifting it into position by the toilet. Becky meanwhile, dared not move as Tatjana had only just settled down and fallen asleep. There were cushions on the floor in front of the washbasin and a grand mess everywhere. Still, ever the good hostess, I was insisting they sit down and have a drink, which they politely declined. In hushed whispers they admired Tatjana as Becky thanked them for their lovely gift. Then they graciously left. I walked them back up to Christine's green convertible with the top down and waved them goodbye. The entire visit was conducted with great decorum. When I returned to the *cave*, Becky said, matter-of-factly, "Do you usually invite your guests to sit on the toilet?" I suppose the answer would be, 'Only on very hot afternoons and only if they are very well dressed.'

Much later that evening, after dinner and a visit up to Montjaux to show the family off, we walked over to see Michel. It was still light at 8.30 in the evening. Tatjana sat papoose style on Daraius' back and off we went – up the drive, down the road to the bridge at Roquetaillade and then the steep climb through the village to Michel's house which had to be the one right at the top.

By car one takes the longer, easier route as you cannot really drive through the village. The road through the centre of the village is extremely narrow, twisty and very, very steep, with a couple of stone archways and stone steps jutting out here and there for good measure. Perhaps a Citroen 2CV would manage it. Whenever we walk through Roquetaillade, we cannot help remembering that on Margaret and

Michael's first visit to this part of the world, long before we arrived, they saw a signpost on the top road saying 'Roquetaillade' and in their big, brown VW camper van made the descent through the village. Once begun, there was no turning back. Down they hurtled, the wing mirrors scraping the walls on the way – never mind the stone arches. They made it, of course, and lived to tell the tale. This incident was probably responsible for two things. One, a signpost in the car park by the bridge pointing away from the village saying *'Toutes directions'* and the other, more intriguingly, a yellow No Parking sign halfway up the village on top of some steep stone steps that are just two feet wide, with a picture of a car being towed away by a very large tow truck.

We got to Michel's, ready for a long cold drink. He was delighted to see us and had obviously had a good 'boy's day out' in Millau with several *pastis* and plenty of wine and was continuing the revelry with a friend. How they drove home in one piece is anybody's guess. He chuckled at Tatjana and made lots of cheery jokes about nothing in particular and told us all about the *Boules* championship. It was beginning to get dark, so Daraius and Becky decided to take Tatjana home and settle her down. They left, with the baby on Becky's back this time, down the steep village road and up the hill after the bridge.

We stayed on for a while listening to Michel. He had, by now, received a phone call from his lady wife admonishing him for not being there when she called, so the conversation naturally veered towards the fairer sex, in particular a glamorous divorcee who had captured his friend's eye. The lady was, apparently, very tall and slim but endowed with an impressive *poitrine*. At this point his friend held his hands out in front of his chest a good way away and rolled his eyes and his hips at the same time, smiling dreamily. "*Comme elle est jolie!*" We did not need any translation.

We left Michel and his drinking partner in an alcoholic haze and headed home. By this time it was pretty dark and all was still. We walked quietly up the road listening to the rustling sounds of night creatures in the bushes and as we rounded the final bend, saw our little house with lights shining through the windows – the only speck of light in a dark, dark valley, except for the stars. Someone else was in there. So this is what it looked like at night to others. It was a strange feeling. We walked down the drive, across the little bridge over the stream and up the stone steps to the front door. The sight that greeted us was one of pure magic. Daraius had lit all the oil lamps, Becky sat with Tatjana sleeping in her arms and there was a glow of what I can only describe as love and warmth all over.

The words that came to mind were 'We've arrived. This is what it's all about'.

****

Four and a half years later, our first granddaughter spent two weeks with us at Joumeyrac. This would be the longest time she'd spent away from her parents and even then, she was confident and secure. She charmed all our friends with her French vocabulary, which extended to *'Bonjour, Merci'* and *'Je voudrais une pomme, s'il vous plait,'* and spent hours gently catching butterflies on the lavender bushes, then letting them go completely unharmed. It was a hot summer and there were plenty of picnics by the river where she learned how to swim, courtesy of Margaret.

We visited the stunning *Abime de Bramabiau*, a grotto discovered by the intrepid Edouard Alfred Martel in 1888. There is an underground river called the *Bonheur,* which flows through the dark and mysterious grotto, only to gush out in an impressive cascade 800 metres further on. The subtle lighting threw long shadows on the rock faces, bringing all the colours to life, and through the eyes of a little girl, this was something out of a fairytale. These were two magical weeks in our lives, even though we could hardly stand up at the end of each day!

Chapter 26: Replacing the Roof DIY

One stormy night in Joumeyrac, we were woken by the sound of dripping water – not just in one place, but several. The red tiled roof was finally showing its age. Something had to be done, and fast. So, we decided to replace the terracotta tiles with new *toisite* tiles, which would be longer lasting and easier to handle. *Toisite* is a composite of bitumen and glass-fibre. *Naturellement*, this being France, we had to apply to the local *Mairie* for a *Permis de Travaux*. The tiles came in two colours – red and grey. We preferred the grey, and now being fully clued-up about French bureaucracy, we requested to have red ones. They insisted we have the grey – this is known as working the system! Having had a couple of half-hearted estimates from local roofers who really didn't want to do it, we thought – 'how hard could it be?' and Jehan made up his mind that we could do it all ourselves, with a bit of help from Michel and Bob. We managed to get the entire month of September off from work, to tackle the project.

The weather was beautiful and dry. We emptied the bedroom and moved everything downstairs or outside, under cover of large tarpaulins. The plan was to work from the inside out as far as possible, leaving the most dangerous part of climbing onto the roof for the very end. Michel arrived and the old red tiles were removed one by one exposing the wooden planks, all of which were rotten. The beams had been attacked by a vicious breed of French ants with very big teeth and were in danger of collapsing. The ants had excavated apartment blocks inside, with amazing precision. Never underestimate an ant. They deserve respect as they can be more destructive than termites.

As soon as the old roof was removed and the house was exposed to the elements it rained of course, in the middle of the night. Fortunately, we had a large tarpaulin in place and the weather cleared the next day.

Then the fun started. Both, Michel and Bob turned up to help. This was indeed very kind of them both, but thanks to some past disagreement many years ago, they did not like each other at all. Added to this, they both had very short fuses and vastly differing opinions on everything, and you can understand what we laid-back individuals were up against!

The climax came when Michel, in trying to fit a beam into the solid stone wall, decided to cut the stone instead of cutting the wood, which seemed to be the obviously easier option. The angle grinder was throwing sparks everywhere, not to mention the dust. We learned lots of French swear words.

Bob, meanwhile, was cutting up the planks of wood with Michel's circular saw and almost sawed off his finger in a fit of anger when the 'Made in China' blades kept going blunt. At one stage, Michel dropped his hammer, narrowly missing Bob. I found the whole circus highly amusing and used all the diplomatic skills I had to keep the peace. Jehan, meanwhile, was doing all the important work and quietly making very good progress on his own.

So, after a week and a half of this skirmish, which might have culminated in murder, we thanked them both profusely for their generosity, tactfully sent them both packing and carried on by ourselves. I am a very good worker's mate and did as I was told while Jehan constructed the roof. We did have a generator for electricity this time, but when it came to putting the tiles on the roof, I had my heart in my mouth most of the time. A strong(ish) hook with a sturdy rope attached was hammered into the apex of the roof and then tied around the old oak tree next to the house. Between the two, it was tied around Jehan's waist. This was supposed to save him if he slipped. I think we both knew it probably wouldn't work should the worst happen, but he was sure he'd be fine, so who was I to argue?

The roof was smoothly and painstakingly accomplished and looks absolutely splendid. It was superbly watertight and also well insulated. Job done.

****

The company Daraius worked for was going from strength to strength and he was asked to set up a new branch in Scotland. He, Becky and Tatjana moved up there in 2004. As ever, he made a success of it and they lived in Carnock for eight years. Harrison was born in 2005 and Xanthia in 2007. We are truly blessed with three gorgeous grandchildren. He is now director of his own firm and they have all moved back to East Sussex now, which is wonderful.

I feel terribly proud that Daraius has taken on the 2nd Hailsham Scout Group and is a Leader with extraordinary talents. They seem to do so much more than we ever did, including the Winter Camp at Gilwell which was Lord Baden-Powell's home. Camping in tents in January – come hail or snow? Thank goodness that had not been on the agenda when I was a cub leader. It's hugely popular and no doubt, very character-building!

Life has always been like a roller coaster. We spent every available holiday in France, interspersed with visits to Italy and occasionally, India, but when we were back home, we did not stop. Both of us were on the committee for the Claygate Village Association and helped to organise all sorts of events throughout the year. We also ran our Fashion shows for charity every

November. There was work and the shop and our family.

By now, with his outstanding musical talents, Jamsheed had a flourishing career as a solo entertainer 'Jamm the Piano Man' on Holland America cruise line. He is very popular and has quite a following, with people booking cruises that he was performing on. Being his oldest and most faithful fans, we thought it made perfect sense to go on one of his cruises! In fact, the first cruise we went on was a special treat from him and we flew to Athens, spending the night in a lovely hotel and joined the cruise the next morning from the port of Piraeus.

The ship was the Ryndam and he had organised a stateroom with a balcony for two weeks. We sailed to Istanbul and visited Corfu, Lesbos, Mykanos and Santorini – places which so far had simply been romantic names. We also stopped at Kusadasi in Turkey and were met by some Turkish friends who took us to Ephesus, which had been a thriving trading port in ancient times. Trading ceased as the river began to silt up over the years and it was finally abandoned, but its grandeur is still evident in the marble pillars and pavements. Excavations are still on-going and they have now found Roman villas with intricate mosaic floors and even paintings on the walls which have been preserved underground for centuries.

Jamm the Piano Man

Jamm the Piano Man and me
entertaining in the Piano Bar.

We also went to Rhodes and Crete, and all the old Greek mythology tales I had read in my youth came to life. The Minotaur, Theseus and Ariadne were here! There is so much to see and learn – several lifetimes would not be enough. The best part of the entire cruise was, of course, getting to listen to our little boy (now very tall and bearded) play the piano and sing every evening in the Piano Bar, surrounded each evening by at least a hundred people who simply adored him. We became celebrities on board the ship when he proudly introduced his parents. One American even asked for my signature....however, it was the same lady who asked if England was the capital of London.

There were other cruises after that, including one from Boston to Montreal, which combined an ocean cruise with a river cruise along the St. Lawrence. We were amazed to find that a great proportion of the population of Quebec and Montreal in Canada, spoke only French. Even menu boards outside Italian restaurants had to be in French. We sailed to Bar Harbour, Halifax in Nova Scotia (where a Scottish piper regaled us), and Prince Edward Island. Boston brought back nostalgic memories of my time there many years ago. It was all simply wonderful. We also managed to be in Canada on 1st of July (Canada Day) and in the USA on the 4th of July, to join in the celebrations.

South Africa featured in our travels, too. This came about through an invitation to a wedding. The young couple were English but had decided to get married in South Africa, and being very close friends of the bride's parents, we were invited. Their wedding was a fairy-tale affair, held at the Grande Provence Estate in Franschhoek. Following the wedding, we spent a few days in Montague and touring the Drakensberg mountains. We also have another dear friend in Somerset (near Cape Town), who had been insisting for several years that we should come and visit. She had just got married and invited us to stay with her and her new husband. Her parents owned several fruit orchards near Stellenbosch, exporting delicious plums, apples and pears all over the world.

This was just the perfect holiday. The weather was stunning every single day. We managed a mini safari, hired a car and drove to Knysna on the Garden Route, walked with baby elephants and visited the Cape of Good Hope, where the mighty Atlantic and Indian Oceans meet. We took in as much as we could, and more. This included a zip wire tree top safari, where we had to sign an indemnity form before they put on our harnesses and sent us off swinging from tree to tree, more than 40 ft above ground level. We were clearly the oldest couple in the group, and the local South African guide, out of respect for his elders, kept calling me 'Mummy', which was highly amusing and thoroughly irritating!!

The Claygate Garden Society organised a trip to the Amalfi Coast in South Italy. We left on my birthday, as it happened, and the first evening at the hotel they produced an amazing cake and sang Happy Birthday! We stayed at Maori and visited several beautiful gardens. One of these was La Mortella, on the island of Ischia, to which we travelled by boat. The name means 'the place of the myrtles' and this exotic, sub-tropical garden, in the sparkling Bay of Naples, was designed by the English composer, Sir William Walton and his Argentinian wife Susana.

We also got to visit the gardens of a private villa in Sorrento, where we were shown round by the owner. She then served us a stupendous tea in her very glamorous kitchen and also sold us a copy of her cookbook. On one of the days when we were allowed to entertain ourselves, Jehan and I hired a little motorboat at Positano and explored along the shore. We wandered quite close to a very sleek and expensive yacht moored a little way out, and the men in black standing guard on deck watched us closely. We were sure they were armed and up to no good. They probably thought we were up to the same.... though we couldn't have got up to much mischief in a hired motor boat. It was a week saturated with beauty, surrounded by friends and thoroughly enjoyable!

One of the spectacular visits organised by the Claygate Gardening Society in 2010 was to the annual tulip festival at Pashley Manor in Sussex. The gardens were awash with magnificent tulips in every colour and variety. Never had I seen such a superb display. (I have not been to Keukenhof in Holland). We were given a guided tour of the gardens and could not resist asking about what happened to the tulips at the end of their season, when they would have to make space for summer bedding. "Why," said the gentleman, " we dig a big hole and get rid of them as we are not allowed to sell them." There was a collective gasp of horror. "However," he continued, "if a charity organisation was willing to come and collect them after we have pulled them up, they would be welcome to have some, as long as the bulbs were planted in public spaces and not in private gardens." Jehan and I promptly volunteered to organise this.

Towards the middle of June, I rang Pashley Manor to ask politely if we could possibly have some tulips to plant in Claygate Village Green. "How many would you like?" asked the lady at the other end of the 'phone line. Hesitantly, I said " Fifty or maybe a hundred? Whatever you can spare." She chuckled and said, "You can have a thousand or as many as you can collect." So, armed with gloves and our large estate car the two of us drove down to Pashley Manor, not knowing what to expect. We were directed to an enormous barn, which was piled high with tulips, complete with leaves, vaguely sorted into heaps of different colours. It smelled like a maturing compost heap. We were told to help ourselves to as many as we liked, so putting the back seats of the car down we crammed it full of fading tulips, the plump bulbs full of promise for the following spring. There were slugs and worms and bits of earth. Thanking Pashley Manor profusely and promising to a put up a plaque on the Green to acknowledge them the following spring, we brought the tulips home and spread them all out under cover in the garden till they dried out thoroughly, cleaned them all up and later that year, along with help from other members of 'Claygate in Bloom' we planted them all over the Village Green. They were brilliant and have been coming up every year without fail. We had been advised to cut the flower heads off the first year before the display started, but we couldn't possibly have brought ourselves to do that!

There was great happiness in all we did. Of course, there were sad and traumatic moments, too, but we had no time to worry about them. We took them in our stride and got on with life. There was always something new and exciting to look forward to around every corner.

Chapter 27: Finding Pont de la Vinzelle

By 2007 the little house in Roquetaillade was getting too small to accommodate the growing family and friends who loved to visit in the summer. It also had its drawbacks with the lack of electricity and mains water. With this in mind, we considered buying another, larger, all singing, all dancing house, not too far from this one. We trawled the internet and one day, Jehan found a picture of a large white house on the edge of what looked like a lake, surrounded by trees and mountains. The price was what we could afford, so it had to be investigated.

We did not receive a reply to our email requesting details, so we sent another one, and several days later there was a response. The owners lived quite far away and the house had been rented out, but was now empty. They were, clearly, not going to come all the way to show the house to someone who wasn't serious about buying it. It was also advertised with a local agent, but we did not know that at the time. A *rendezvous* was made for the middle of June and we flew to Rodez, in the Aveyron, for three days. We also went and saw some other houses through a local agent, but this one had already captured our imagination.

It was on the right bank of the river Lot. The house was on high ground, set well back from the road. Across the road were fields of meticulously tended lettuces, in every colour and variety. The fields stretched down to the river, with fifteen or so walnut trees along the edge. There were cherry trees further down, laden with fruit, and more vegetables. This land came with the house, but had been rented out to a market gardener. The house needed a lot of work to make it comfortable, but that is exactly what we wanted – another holiday project! What was more, this house had a fantastic water source, which produced 13 litres a minute throughout the year. There was also mains water available but one did not need it.

However, when I mentioned drainage and sewers, the owner shrugged her shoulders and said "*Non.*" Then she explained, nonchalantly "*Dans la riviere,*" waving her hand over her shoulder. We were horrified. This was, of course, quite common in France. It was imperative that we install a *fosse septique* as soon as possible, although this did not seem urgent to the vendors at all. However, for us, this would be the first priority, and, having bought the house, we had it done professionally at great expense. The next job was to remove the central heating system. Why? You ask.

Well, it was a wood fired system. The stove for burning the wood was large enough to roast a whole pig and built on a plinth of bricks, which you almost tripped over as you entered the house. It occupied half the room. Leading from the stove were large water pipes, which carried hot water to the radiators all round the house. These were, in turn, enormous and very old. The entire ensemble looked like the interior of the engine room on the Queen Mary. This time, we hired local labour to remove the lot. Then, with a blank canvas, we got stuck in.

The false ceiling in the large room downstairs came down to expose the beams. All the ancient wiring fell down too, along with desiccated mice and the debris of the ages. Jehan spent a long time rewiring the entire house. Two enormous beams had to be replaced, as there was extensive damage from ancient termites. As one of these beams was holding up the staircase, it was a bit urgent. Two sturdy carpenters from the local joinery came and accomplished this between them. The other rotten beam was propping up a heavy, square stone, which might have been used as a fireplace for the upstairs. This done, I set to work painting everything white.

There was a double garage next to the house and it was clear that someone had been using it while the house had been unoccupied. The day we arrived, we had the pleasure of meeting our one and only neighbour. He only spoke French (perfectly logical, this), and was delighted that we spoke French, too. Jean-Pierre and his wife Nathalie lived in the valley behind our property in a beautifully converted walnut oil mill. The powerful force of water in the Vinzelle river, which cascaded down the mountainside into the Lot, had been harnessed, many years ago, to turn a huge grindstone, which crushed the walnuts to produce walnut oil. The mill had been in use right up to 1962. Jean-Pierre is a man after our own hearts and never happier than when he is busy creating something out of nothing. We struck up a great relationship and they are the neighbours from heaven, much like our neighbours Carole and Barry, in Claygate. We could not ask for more. Add to this, that they had a superb swimming pool, which was at our disposal whenever we liked. We were truly delighted.

Thanks to JP, who introduced us to Serge, the local baker, who is also a very useful handyman and knew just about everybody, we soon made new friends. Serge lives in a mill, too. This was originally a watermill by the river, for grinding wheat. It seems appropriate that Serge bakes bread in an old wood-fired stone oven every Thursday. He has clients who come from miles around to buy his bread, which remains edible for up to ten days. (Here I must add that it is as chewy on the first day as on the last), but has a fascinating addictive quality, nevertheless.

Throughout the year, whenever we turn up, Stefan, our market gardener, brings an enormous box of seasonal vegetables for us. They grow practically everything, including tomatoes and cucumbers in their enormous greenhouses. Twice a week, they take their produce to a wholesale market in Aurillac. It is a family business, and they work very hard. One day, I decided I would help a couple of the ladies with harvesting beans. It was trickier than I thought, as they had to be picked absolutely perfectly because they were going to the market. I also discovered a little grass snake having a nap among the rows. This caused great excitement, as none of us were sure that it wasn't a viper. I do wear garden gloves for everything now!

The house was coming along beautifully. Jamsheed came down with us in the first year to help lay a wooden floor. This was quite an operation and we hired a van from England, stopped in Orleans to buy the wooden flooring, as it was well priced, and drove down. It was lovely and transformed the house. Jehan made new wooden shutters, with the help of electricity this time, for the awkwardly shaped windows and we painted the upstairs shutters lavender blue. To us, this was the traditional French look, but it now appears that all the houses with blue shutters in the Aveyron belong to Brits!

The village of La Vinzelle is perched on top of the mountain behind our house. There is a charming mountain trail to walk up to it. This trail used to be the main road and goes right past our house, which used to be a trading post and an inn, where people would stop for the night. They would sleep in a dormitory on the first floor (now partitioned into four bedrooms). The river was the main means of transport and goods would arrive from far and wide. They were transported up to La Vinzelle by bullock-cart. Just like in India! Happily, a local man has written a book about his boyhood in this area and our house is pictured in it, as it was at the turn of the century.

There is an amusing story about the landlady of the inn. Locals would come and drink there and run up a tab, often not paying on time. She would write all their names and how much they owed, in big letters, on a very visible notice inside the *armoire,* (the cupboard behind the bar), and when necessary, open the doors of the cupboard and name and shame them in front of everyone. There was also the illegal practice of fishing by torchlight – the fish come to the surface and are easier to catch. The local *gendarmerie* turned a blind eye to this as they enjoyed their drinks on the house. More recently, one of the tenants, who was infamous for his drinking habits decided to go torchlight fishing one night while thoroughly inebriated and fell into the river. That was when the house became vacant.

Pont de la Vinzelle was made habitable and very comfortable, with not one, but two new bathrooms and all manner of modern conveniences. There is plenty of space for friends and family and many places of interest to visit nearby. The scenery along the river is fantastic in every season and best of all, there is an ice cream parlour within a short walking distance with a playground, for the grandchildren.

In 2007 Jehan became a Parish Councillor for Claygate. It was a great commitment and took up most of his time, but always interesting. The only problem was that as I had a shop in the middle of the village, every complaint there was to be made by anyone was delivered to us in person. The other nine councillors were not quite so accessible. This often led to a bit of stress, as some people did not seem to understand that the shop was nothing to do with the Parish Council! However, being the hub of social activity in Claygate was always good fun. People came to us for advice on all sorts of matters, from health to relationships! We were already in the process of planning the second Music Festival for 2008.

This turned out to be an even greater success than the first one, with all kinds of music over the two weeks. We hosted a famous London orchestra, two terrific choirs, a very popular Jazz band and a Big Swing Band amongst others. Each alternate year, we organised a Garden Trail in the village, when certain residents would open their pretty gardens for charity. This was also a big undertaking and took up any spare time. It was always a popular event, as it really got the community together. Of course, it was hard work for the gardeners, who were under pressure to make their garden perfect, but the pleasure they gave to the visitors and the appreciation they received, must have made it all worthwhile. Claygate also has an annual Flower Show, which is just about the only committee we were not on! This has been a very long-standing event and very well established and seems to get busier each year.

In 2009, we were also helping to organise 'Claygate in Bloom' for the RHS South East in Bloom competition. This was a major event. The village was spruced up, tubs planted, pavements weeded, signposts cleaned and repaired. The judges were arriving on the 8th of July 2009. On Tuesday the 7th preparations had to be made to set up displays in the Village Hall. It was a beautiful morning. Jehan had been in the shop earlier that morning and then went home to sort some things out to take to the Village Hall. Half an hour later, I received a 'phone call. "Sweetie, please come home straightaway."

Panic-stricken, I picked up my bag, locked the shop and ran home. I was there in under two minutes. There, doubled up in pain, turning blue and sweating profusely, was my healthy, active husband in the full throes of a heart attack. He kept insisting it was indigestion but I immediately put in a 999 call. The Rapid Response medic just happened to be in the vicinity and was there within seconds. The ambulance turned up shortly after. Meanwhile, I had rung my neighbours and they were, of course, wonderful. I went to Kingston Hospital with him in the ambulance, never once thinking he may never come back. The darkest moment for me was sitting outside the theatre while they assessed his situation. All I could see was the heart monitor, which was mercifully producing little blips. Then I was told they had to rush him to St. George's Hospital in Tooting, as they did not have the facilities at Kingston to perform the stent procedure, which he desperately needed.

With the blue light flashing and sirens blaring, the paramedics got us to St. George's in minutes. They were ready for him and I then spent the longest half-hour of my life, waiting for news. It was truly wonderful when they finally called me in to see him. I had rung Jamsheed, who was in Brighton at the time and he had rushed up as soon as he could.

The day before, Daraius had left with the family for our house in France, where we were to join them the following week. There was no point alarming him as there would be little they could have done. When all was well, I did ring and tell him 'Dad had a little heart attack' but before I did that, I made sure Jehan was well enough to talk to Daraius himself! After a short stay in hospital, Jehan was home and recovering very well. We thought we'd have to cancel going to France, but he cheerfully assured me that the doctor said it was fine to drive. I did not believe that for an instant, so insisted on driving, if indeed we did go at all. I was permitted to drive to Dover and the first bit in France, but after that all went back to normal.

This would be a good point to thank all our wonderful friends who came to our aid, especially Soonu and Dins who took Jamsheed and me under their wing from day one. There was a lot of support from our dear neighbours, Pam and David and Carole and Barry, and a lot of other people and we appreciated it all very much. Nor will I hear any criticism of our National Health Service. We are incredibly lucky in Britain to have such an efficient and well-organised emergency service. The paramedics were amazing and the nurses very kind. We have also learned to value ourselves a bit more and not take on too many tasks at once. Life can be very short. We have been lucky.

****

A few years after this, in April 2012, to be precise, we were in France again, having flown down and looking forward to using our latest acquisition, a French registered Fiat Ulysse, which we had bought second-hand from the local garage. It was a 7 seater people carrier with a high roof and in terrific condition. The tyres were new, the battery was new, and we'd had the registration and MOT done at great expense. It was dark green.

The weather was typical of April and there had been a lot of rain prior to our visit. The ground was saturated. The day after our arrival, we set off for the market in Rodez and bought plants and flowers to jolly up the front of the house. We also filled up the huge petrol tank. It was a very windy day and on the way back we were delayed, thanks to a huge tree that had come crashing down in the wind, blocking the road. Our local farmers were in the process of chain-sawing it to remove the obstruction. We stopped to chat and then went on our way, saying how fortunate it was that nobody had been hurt.

Five minutes later and only 50 metres from our house, there was the most horrendous bang – like a double decker bus landing on top of us. An enormous oak tree had chosen exactly that moment to fall and it landed squarely on top of our car, smashing the windscreen, the bonnet and the roof directly above our heads. We were covered in glass and completely shocked. Both of us thought we were dead, as nothing hurt and there was no blood. This must be what it's like to die suddenly – no pain. We looked at each other in disbelief and said 'Are you alright?' then, 'Yes, are *you* alright?' I gingerly opened my door, which practically fell off its hinges, with more glass everywhere. We were amidst huge branches and foliage. The roof of the car had missed our heads by an inch. We were totally unscathed but shaking like leaves.

Of course, help was at hand immediately and everyone was amazed that we were still in one piece. We walked home and in a state of shock I think we ate a banana. We were so thankful at being alive and well, that not once have we had nightmares about it – Jehan's only grouse was the 80 Euros worth of petrol he'd just filled it up with!

The car also had only third party insurance on it, and the tree being the third party and on council land, we were assured it was an 'act of God' and that was that. So, no material compensation but hey, all we lost was an expensive chunk of metal! We're alive, and now realise more than ever that life is for living and enjoying and making the most of. That's what really matters.

Chapter 28: One House Less in the Aveyron

The next couple of years went by in a haze of shop work, fashion shows, music festivals and several trips to France. We still had the little house, as it cost us only the yearly taxes and no other bills. Many years ago, we had bought another acre of land in the valley nearby with a little stone ruin on it. It was by a bend in the river and was ideal agricultural land. We'd never had the time to do anything with it, so finally, in 2013 we decided to advertise it on the internet and sell it. Having no idea of the market value, we made up a price and waited. There were several time wasters, but one French lady constantly sent us emails saying she was definitely going to buy it. Well, nobody does that without seeing the place first. We ignored her as a crackpot. She persisted, and then one morning, I received a 'phone call at the shop. It was her, asking if we had received and understood her messages. I said that we had and we did, but couldn't imagine she was serious. She explained that she had managed to locate the land from all the pictures we had sent, that it was like a dream come true for her and she was going to buy it. So, we made a *rendezvous* to meet her on our next visit to Joumeyrac.

At the agreed hour, we arrived at the bar in St. Rome de Tarn and ordered a coffee. We looked round for the lady. From her name and the conversations over the 'phone, we had imagined that she would be an outdoor farmer type – rather plain, large and hearty. There was nobody fitting that description. However, over in the far corner, there was a rather glamorous, slim young woman, with a notebook and dark glasses, smiling at us. We hit it off straightaway. She was an accomplished musician and a psychotherapist, married with five children and a first grandchild. Her ambition was to create a Garden of Peace on our land, where she could bring some of her patients to relieve their stress. In her notebook, she had already planned the layout of the garden. She had also made a note of what trees there already were on the land, and the new ones she would be planting. It was a very impressive brief and we went to the *Notaire's* office immediately to talk business.

By the time we returned to France a couple of months later, the garden was well under way. Her husband had been roped in to help of course, but most of the work had been done by her. Some nights, she would sleep in a tent on this remote piece of land, with only her trusty dog, Shadow, for company. She seemed very happy with her project and we have become good friends over the years. We take an English plant to add to her garden on every trip. What an amazing lady. She also had her eye on Joumeyrac, so if we ever wanted to sell it, it would be in good hands.

We thought about the future quite a lot, as most of our friends had already retired and were enjoying life and spending more time with their families. It was time to make a few changes in our lives. So we started to think about closing the shop. After eighteen years of hugely successful trading and building up a wonderful customer base, we decided that it was now or never. We did not want to wait until ill health or boredom forced us to close.

Our loyal customers were horrified and the entire village was devastated, as this shop had been the 'Village Well' where everyone came to shop, gossip and cheer themselves up over a cup of coffee and a joke or two. Nearly every event in the village was either organised by us, or even if it wasn't, we knew chapter and verse about it and were always there to help. We had convinced ourselves that family came first. Daraius and his lovely family lived in Hailsham, near Eastbourne, and Jamsheed lived in Brighton. Both sons thought it would be a good idea for us to sell up and move closer to them. We thought it would be a good idea, too. To begin with, we would be very useful for baby-sitting and general support but many years from now, they would be useful to baby-sit us!! (Let's hope it never comes to that)!

So, we closed the shop and continued the business with pop-up shops at the Village Hall and at home, which meant that I got to meet all my lovely customers and still keep in touch. There will be a time when that will stop, too. We also started looking at moving to East Sussex.

The biggest wrench of all would be leaving our dear neighbours and various wonderful friends of thirty-four years. Our children had been at school together and many happy times had been enjoyed – fancy dress parties, New Year's Eve parties (especially one where we all dressed like cavemen and did the Conga around the Green), firework nights, bonfires in back gardens, going to each other's houses when we were all snow-bound and sharing mulled wine and mince pies – too many wonderful times to mention. Then we would think of our future generation growing up not knowing much about their grandparents and things would come into perspective. After all, the south coast was only an hour and a bit away!

Our house in Claygate went on the market in October 2014. We started to house-hunt seriously and set our sights on the village of Heathfeld. In fact, having looked at several properties, we finally found one we liked, although it did not tick all the boxes. We had an offer on our house so there was some urgency to find somewhere. As it happened, our buyers changed their mind so we pulled out of our prospective purchase, which was just as well. A couple of weeks later we had another, much better offer which was accepted. This time we thought we'd explore closer to Eastbourne, and decided to look at a house that had only just come onto the market in the village of Polegate. Along with our friends Maggie and Rick, we arrived at the house, walked in, and we all went

'AAAAAH!' That was it. Without investigating the village, the neighbours, the distance from the shops or anything else, for that matter, we made an offer that very same afternoon.

The offer was accepted immediately and it was all systems go. We then found that there was a very pleasant high street with all the services you could want within walking distance, a railway station with lines to London and Gatwick airport and the location was superb. As for the house, it had been completely renovated top to bottom in the best possible taste. The bi-fold patio doors opened up onto a fair-sized garden, beyond which were open fields and the South Downs National Park. This meant that it was not overlooked in any way and there was no chance of that land being developed in the future. Every so often, there are black-headed sheep that graze in the field directly behind the house.

The final completion date was the 12th of June 2015 and we moved from Claygate to Polegate. The biggest pantechnicon you ever saw and a second lorry brought our entire worldly contents down. There is nothing quite as sobering as moving house. It puts you in touch with your materialistic self and you suddenly realise that you do not need (and probably have never really needed) half the stuff you have accumulated over the years. In spite of several trips to the tip and the charity shops, there was so much that came with us! We are still clearing out. I'm sure I speak for most of the sheds in the country that are packed with bits of wood, half cans of paint and leftover bits of plastic guttering. They do indeed, come in useful, but only if you remember you have them when you need them! And, having remembered, only if you ever find them.

2015 was busier than usual. Having moved to Polegate in June, we decided to succumb to our lovely French lady's request to buy Joumeyrac. We really did not need two houses in France and it was becoming hard work looking after the little one, as we could not spend enough time there. It was far better to sell it to someone who was going to love it and look after it. So, in August, we made a rendezvous with Madame and the *Notaire* and started the ball rolling. After the initial *Compromis de vente* was signed, we gave her the keys, which was highly irregular, as the final *Acte de Vente* would not be signed until October when all the finances would be completed. However, all was fine, as expected, and when we arrived in October, we had never seen the house looking so smart, clean and happy. Joumeyrac had clearly found a soul-mate.

The only piece of furniture we removed from Joumeyrac was an old oak dining table, which had been given to us by our lovely neighbours Barry and Carole in Claygate many years ago. I had used it as a cutting table when I worked from home, then used it in the shop and finally took it to Joumeyrac. It is now back in

England, proudly residing in Daraius and Becky's house in Hailsham. A historical and very lovely table! If only pieces of furniture could talk, what tales they would tell.

Our family continues to give us great pleasure. Thanks to their brilliant parents, with a dedicated mid-wife for a mother, all three grandchildren are an absolute joy, and much loved. They are all thoroughly musical, with Tatjana playing the flute and also the piano and Harry playing the guitar. Xanthia and Harry are exceptional gymnasts in their own fields and Tatjana's mathematical and artistic skills are impressive. Apart from which, they are all endowed with a superb sense of humour (except when they are sulking, of course). We cannot ask for more. I could ask for Harry to tell me how he does his card tricks, but, as he says 'A good Magician never tells his secrets'. I wonder what they will be when they grow up – I suspect that at least one of them will write a book!

With some of the proceeds from the sale of Joumeyrac, we decided to treat Pont de la Vinzelle to new double glazed windows and doors. We were amazed at the very reasonable quote given to us by a local *menuisier* who took the measurements accurately and said they would accomplish the job in November. In typical French style, they did not respond to our emails asking to confirm dates and times, so we had no idea if they were on the ball or not. However, we went down in November and hey presto – 8 am on Monday morning saw four burly workmen arrive complete with windows and door.

They worked from 8 till 12, stopped for lunch, then 2 till 6 non-stop. No tea breaks, no *pastis* breaks, no loud radio and cheeky banter. By Tuesday evening, all ten windows and the door were replaced and everything was back to normal, clean and tidy. Very impressive, indeed. To top it all, they did not bill us for another five days, so we thought they might charge more than the original estimate. But no, it was exactly the same price, so we paid it all with a big smile and a big box of chocolates.

To round off a most exciting year, we were invited by the Claygate Village Association to switch on the Christmas lights for 2015. This invitation was a surprise and a great honour for us, and was extended by way of a 'Thank You' for all the events we had started and organised in Claygate over the past 34 years. It was a fun event and we felt hugely appreciated and missed! The whole family came up for the event and the entire village had turned out (or so it seemed)! We were given a Certificate of Appreciation, a large bottle of champagne, the most beautiful bouquet and to top it all, a very posh purple watering-can with a brass plaque saying 'With love from Claygate'. There are several people I can think of, who deserve this sort of accolade but as they still live in Claygate, I expect nobody notices! It's a bit like hearing all about someone's lifetime achievements at their funeral and thinking 'Gosh, I had no idea – wish I'd known that when he/she was alive'.

There are so many people in so many towns, who do enormous amounts of voluntary work for their communities – simply out of community spirit. They should all be highly respected and better still, supported all the way.

With all the troubles the world is going through (as it always has since time immemorial), it is good to know that there are many more good people than bad everywhere. It's just that the media thinks we get more excited about bad news and if they constantly gave out good news, it might become boring. There are many situations that we common people can do nothing about, so the best policy has to be to look after your own patch, your own village, your own community and do your best to make things happy in your own small bubble. If everyone did that, the world's problems would be solved. Sounds simplistic, but it is achievable!

Life is now supposed to be slowing down for us, but hey, we've just retired! This is a new beginning and there is plenty waiting to be done and lovely new people to meet and places to see. But that will have to be another chapter in another book. We have gone full circle and now Daraius has invited us on a family holiday to Marrakech! He and Becky know it well and want to share it with the children and us. This will be a wonderful new adventure, and we are very excited. However, that will have to be another chapter in another book. So, roll on, Marrakech!

That's All, Folks!

Acknowledgements and Thanks to

My great-great grandmother, Dosebai Cawasjee Jessawalla for the inspiration to write this book, having read the story of her life.

My grandparents Tehmina and Jamshedji Cama.

My parents Mani and Nozer Homji for all the family history they wrote down and told me.

My sister Feroza for nagging me to get on with it.

My brilliant husband Jehan for always being there with his patience, encouragement and technical skills.

Margaret and Michael Clark for encouragement to write my life story.

Charles Cooper for proof-reading with diligence and interest and Barbara Cooper for putting up with it all with very good humour.

Maggie and Rick for encouragement and help all the way and to each and every one of our lovely friends who have made our lives extra special with their love and kindness.

Thank You

Lightning Source UK Ltd.
Milton Keynes UK
UKHW020613091019
351249UK00006B/29/P